Praise for *The FUSE Pathway*

"I have watched Paul live this book over the twenty-four years since I first walked into his studio. We met at a drawing workshop I was teaching, and Paul invited me to visit his studio over the lunch break. That first encounter with Dulcinea, his painting machine, started conversations on Renaissance painting, composition, and analyses of Old Master paintings, which continued in museums all over Europe as Paul joined me on nine different sketching tours. Each trip added concepts that turned into computer code in the hands of an artist-engineer, combining what many would consider to be mutually exclusive. Paul's life is the best example of his book, living a life of purposeful enjoyment in discovery and creativity."

—**Glenn Vilppu**, visual artist and instructor, Vilppu Academy

"*The Fuse Pathway* offers a fresh perspective on merging seemingly opposite passions, allowing you to be true to all parts of yourself. Paul Kirby shares real-life stories and a helpful framework to help you weave your interests into a fulfilling lifestyle. Dive into this book if you are ready to embrace the extraordinary essence of your life."

—**Thea Rotteveel**, corporate consultant, coach, and author of *First-Choice Life*

The *FUSE* Pathway

How to Find and Live a Fulfilling Life

PAUL KIRBY

GREENLEAF
BOOK GROUP PRESS

Published by Greenleaf Book Group Press
Austin, Texas
www.gbgpress.com

Distributed by Greenleaf Book Group

For ordering information or special discounts for bulk purchases, please contact Greenleaf Book Group at PO Box 91869, Austin, TX 78709, 512.891.6100.

Design and composition by Greenleaf Book Group
Cover design by Greenleaf Book Group and Jonathan Lewis
Cover images used under license from ©adobestock.com/Yuliana
Photography by Shadow Play Films and Human Design

Publisher's Cataloging-in-Publication data is available.

Print ISBN: 979-8-88645-263-1

eBook ISBN: 979-8-88645-264-8

To offset the number of trees consumed in the printing of our books, Greenleaf donates a portion of the proceeds from each printing to the Arbor Day Foundation. Greenleaf Book Group has replaced over 50,000 trees since 2007.

Printed in China on acid-free paper

25 26 27 28 29 30 31 32. 10 9 8 7 6 5 4 3 2 1

First Edition

To future fusioneers: May you lead fulfilling lives,
as you were meant to live.

Fusioneering:

Combining two or more of your interests and passions to create a vision and way of life that is more in line with your true purpose.

Contents

Foreword

My father enlisted in the military after college, following the bombing of Pearl Harbor. That's when he met my mother, a civilian who worked as a typist in a medical military facility. He was impressed with how fast she could type and how easily she could spell long medical terms. He pursued her, and she agreed to write to him. They exchanged letters, even though it took three months for one's letter to reach the other by military transport. When my father left for the war in the Pacific, my mother joined the WAAC (Women's Army Auxiliary Corps). She eventually spent her time in the European theater, landing at Normandy about a month after the invasion. When the war ended, they married. They liked the military life, so my father continued on as a career army officer. That meant they—and, eventually, we—moved often. I was born in the United States but spent several years growing up in Austria and Denmark.

As a kid, I made some friends, but not being able to speak the language, I learned how to entertain myself and spent a lot of time alone. Being a shy kid, that was perfectly fine with me. I always liked building things with my hands. I spent hours with my Lincoln Logs, Erector set, and Tinker Toys. Whenever I got in trouble, my mom could never discipline me by sending me to my room because that wasn't a punishment for me. That love for building things stayed

William R. Hewlett, president of Hewlett-Packard, and seventeen-year-old Paul

with me as I grew up. Later, we moved to the Bay Area in Northern California. One summer, my best friend and I made a chemistry set so we could analyze rock samples. It wasn't part of any class; we just did it because we were curious.

I may have been shy, but I was always a self-starter. During my sophomore year in high school, I joined the Junior Achievement program. It was a group of fifteen kids from different schools in the area who met once a week. We formed a company of our own, elected a president, then made a product we went around town trying to sell. I was elected president three years in a row and was even President of the Year in Santa Clara County, so I got to go to the national competition. That really helped me distinguish myself.

Each year, the Junior Achievement companies were sponsored by a real company. Hewlett-Packard sponsored my company during my senior year in 1968. While taking a tour of their headquarters in Palo

Alto, I saw a sign above a door in the hallway that said "employment," so I popped in to ask for a summer job application. I was looking for a simple job and would have done anything, but they must have seen my potential. I had been accepted at Cal Berkeley and planned to major in engineering. My Junior Achievement sponsor probably put in a good word for me as well, because I wasn't given just any summer job. I was hired to work in Hewlett-Packard's prestigious corporate research lab.

Every morning, I rode my bike nine miles from Mountain View to Palo Alto. I was assigned to work for James Rudolph, one of the section managers at the lab. He was a great boss and would give me open-ended assignments to see what I could do. I'd just run with it. I had my own engineering cubicle and filled it with all sorts of HP instruments and electronic parts. Sometimes I was assigned to a team, and we worked together, but it was all very unstructured. I'd spend the entire summer tinkering, working with my hands, and figuring things out. Most days, I'd work well into the evening before riding my bike home. I always missed dinner, so my mom kept it in the oven, but that didn't bother me. I was working all the time, and I loved it.

Everyone working at the lab had a PhD and was at the top of their field. It was the crème de la crème. We spent time together and would chat in the cafeteria during lunch, but they never treated me like a kid. In the beginning, they taught me about circuits and how to solder. One engineer helped me tune up the metal detector I had made and used on the beach.

Each year, HP kept hiring me back, even in an economic downturn, and I worked there four summers in a row. I found out years later that it was Bill Hewlett himself who hired me. One day, he just walked into the lab managers' weekly staff meeting and said, "I hired this kid for the summer. Who wants him?" Jim said he'd take me, and I'm glad he did, because that gave me experience I couldn't get in college, and those summers paid for my college education.

Jim and I remained lifelong friends, and we swapped Christmas letters until 2022, when his letter was returned to me. I saw in the obituaries that he had passed away, and it hit me hard.

Along with Stanford and MIT, Berkeley was one of the top three engineering schools in the country, but the classes were all theoretical. Some of the math and science classes were challenging, and I certainly learned a lot, but I spent my time in the classroom with textbooks. I still preferred working with my hands to design and build things.

The ongoing war in Vietnam soon changed everything for me. On December 1, 1969, the military held the first draft lottery drawing since 1942. Birthdays were picked at random on national television. Those with the birthdays picked first would be the first to serve. My birthday was selected twelfth.

I still had two years remaining at Berkeley, but without a student deferment, I didn't have much choice. The lab manager at HP wanted me to get my master's in electrical engineering at nearby Stanford and become a conscientious objector. "I can't do that," I told him. Both of my parents served in the military. I felt I had a responsibility and duty. That was that.

The Air Force ROTC was accepting eighteen pilot and engineering candidates. I applied and was accepted. I attended basic training in the summer after my sophomore year, prior to the two-year program in school. After graduating from Cal Berkeley in 1972, I was commissioned as a second lieutenant and reported for active duty on August 15 at Lowry Air Force Base in Denver. I was assigned to a research laboratory and given a military specialty code of "computer system design engineer." Then I was temporarily assigned to a military school elsewhere to become a research and development contracting officer.

My research lab was managing a multimillion-dollar R&D contract with McDonnell Douglas. We were developing a prototype state-of-the-art training system of the future for a couple

Lowry Air Force Base front gate

thousand enlisted men and women on my base. The idea was to improve training by making it more efficient while also making it more cost-effective by shortening the training pipeline. This was years before the advent of the personal computer, so we had a giant CDC supercomputer housed in our lab on the base. Back then, it was so big that it filled a large room and lay on a raised floor above its gigantic cooling system. We laid miles of cable around the base, connecting our supercomputer to participating classrooms in this test program. The idea was to semiautomate a few trial courses that ranged in variety from logistics to loading nuclear bombs on to B-52s.

Given my background and work experience, I was able to create unique solutions to problems. One was a device to collect and store information about power outages, which showed a correlation to when the supercomputer crashed. This resulted in the contractor installing a massive battery backup system. Another was an electronic device to automate an aspect of our educational system, for which I received a US patent on behalf of the Air Force. With these successes within our own lab, I was able to set up my own electronic shop with a technician to assist me.

The Air Force major I reported to in the lab had a PhD in electrical engineering. It became apparent he had no hands-on experience, through no fault of his own. Because I had worked at HP Labs, I knew how to design, build, and wire circuits, which included the ability to solder intricate components. Had I just gone to Berkeley, with no experience at HP Labs, I might never have learned how to accomplish what I did. I later learned that my replacement wasn't able to do any of that. When you have multiple skill sets, it changes your perspective. It allows you to see problems in a different light and approach the solution from different angles.

I enjoyed my four years in the Air Force and received two commendation medals for technical contributions. I gained valuable experience there, but ever since participating in Junior Achievement in high school, I knew I wanted to earn an electrical engineering degree and an MBA. During my senior year at Cal Berkeley, I was accepted to Harvard Business School. I knew that finding a job after graduating from Harvard would be easier than getting a job out of the Air Force, so it was an easy decision. The GI Bill covered a third of my tuition and room and board. I had saved up enough money to pay for a third, and I took out student loans for the final third.

It would be at Harvard where my life changed in many profound ways. It is also where the seed for my fulfilling and extensive fusioneering journey was planted.

Paul and Dulcinea, his robot, creating a new painting

INTRODUCTION

The Fusioneering Framework

"I am not a painter! I'm a fusioneer!" I blurted to Lauren, an art consultant who was trying to talk me into selling my paintings. It was the first time I'd ever used the term *fusioneer*. And it was born out of frustration. As you'll read, she knew I was more than a painter, having combined—or fused—many of my interests and passions in pursuit of my own, unique vision.

In 2014, Lauren had made two visits to my studio in Loveland, Colorado, and I had given her an immersive tour. I walked her through my creative process and told her the story behind each painting on display. We spent hours discussing why I do what I do, but we weren't on the same page. She saw the abstract paintings on the walls of my studio but paid little attention to the fact that I had not created them on my own or in any traditional way.

My artistic partner was Dulcinea, a ten-by-ten-foot robot I had spent nine years building. Dulcinea not only made every single

Paul in his studio with his oil paintings, computers, and robot

brushstroke but cleaned her own brush, changed paint colors, sealed the jars, and even turned off her own power when she was done for the night. She was fully automated and could work unattended. Each painting required meticulous planning and thousands of lines of code, but Dulcinea was much more than a glorified printer. She made spontaneous, unexpected, and exquisite brushstrokes that gave each of these completely original pieces of art such emotional depth. *She* was responsible for the magic.

Approaching seventy years old and nearing the end of my career, I hired Lauren to help me figure out what I was going to do with Dulcinea, my studio, the paintings, and everything I had spent twenty-eight years building after I was gone. She had helped an artist friend of mine sell his paintings and came highly recommended, but I wasn't interested in selling my paintings. My contract with her was to strategize a way forward. It can take months to a few years to create just one painting. Each of them is special to me, and too valuable to me to sell. Lauren refused to accept that.

Dulcinea creating beautiful brushstrokes

With relief, she and I shortly parted ways. However, I still didn't have an answer for what I would do with the paintings and my studio. So I simply followed my energy and went back to work. A few years later, I created a website with a collection of short video clips showcasing Dulcinea, my work, and the paintings. Every so often, a few close friends would visit, but I was content just following my dream of fusing art and science.

In 2018, one of those friends, Bill Moninger, told me he knew a local teacher interested in bringing some of her gifted fourth- and fifth-grade students over to see my studio. I asked if they could briefly look at my website ahead of time, just so they'd understand what they were walking into. I assumed they wouldn't do that, but I was wrong.

Bill and I were standing on the sidewalk outside my studio to greet the teacher and her students when they arrived. As Bill introduced me to the teacher, the kids heard my name and went bonkers! They ran around in circles, yelling and screaming, arms flailing. Never before had anyone been so excited to meet me. I was like a rock star.

I ushered everyone inside, and the kids got even more excited as they looked at my robot and the paintings on the walls, but as soon as I started to talk, they went dead silent. I had their undivided attention. They had two gears: pure excitement and complete, focused concentration. After I talked about my process and explained the story behind the paintings, we all sat in a semicircle on the floor. That's when one of the kids asked me a thoughtful question: "Do you like painting more or working with the robot?"

"I don't have to choose," I told him. "Because of Dulcinea, I can do both. Let's say that you really like apple pie, and you also like—" I was about to say, "vanilla ice cream," but before I could even get the words out, the kids all shouted it out in unison with such enthusiasm. Having seen the short video on my website, they already knew what I was going to say. Many of the people who had previously visited the studio would either relate to the paintings and ignore the robot or relate to the robot and ignore the paintings. These kids were enthusiastic for both. On a fundamental level, they intuitively understood what I did.

If you like apple pie and vanilla ice cream, you don't have to pick one or the other. You can put them together to create something new that is more than the sum of its parts: apple pie à la mode. That is what I struggled to articulate to Lauren and so many of the other people I've met over the years who asked me why I didn't just paint. The reason was because it would limit me. I love art and painting, but I also love conceptualizing a new painting, figuring out how I'm going to create it, writing code, and utilizing some AI techniques, making things in the machine shop, and collaborating with Dulcinea on the design, brushwork, and color to eventually bring it all to life. This is what I call my "fusion space," where all these disciplines come together. That's where I truly love to be.

Those kids got it, and their energy was infectious. That moment had a profound impact on me, and it helped to solidify the answer I had been seeking about what to do with my work. It would be great if one of my paintings wound up on the wall of a famous museum, but that wouldn't tell the whole story. The understanding of what went on behind the canvas and what it meant to be a fusioneer would be missing. What I really wanted to do was share my story and give back. I wanted people to see what I've done and feel inspired to pursue their own dreams. That was the missing component, and that became the ultimate goal. From that point forward, I had a new mission and dharmic meaning in my life.

The Fusioneering Spectrum

Once I could define the concept for myself, I could recognize other fusioneers throughout history who expanded boundaries and broke new ground. What's great about fusioneering is that there isn't only one way to do it, and there isn't only one type of fusioneer. There is a broad spectrum that can be broken down into four distinct types.

Fusion: Combining Two or More Interests

The first type of fusioneering is simple. It involves combining your interests into a domain that is new to you. For example, you could be a writer who loves to write and also loves to travel. You can simply combine those two passions to become a travel writer. You're not breaking new ground, but that doesn't matter if you can do what you love and aren't forced to choose one pursuit.

Born in Brookline, Massachusetts, but raised in Corvallis, Oregon, in the 1960s and 1970s, Jon Krakauer was an avid reader. Although he never studied writing, he dreamed about one day becoming a writer, but that dream was temporarily put on hold. His love of the outdoors and mountaineering occupied most of his time and energy. After graduating from Hampshire College with a degree in environmental studies, he spent three weeks alone in the Alaskan wilderness. He worked part-time as a fisherman and carpenter. He was finally able to fuse his love of writing with the outdoors when he became a journalist for *Outside*.

Krakauer didn't create a new domain. This type of nonfiction writing existed long before he started writing, but it was new to him. Most important, it allowed him to combine two things that he loved. He soon branched out to other publications while never turning his back on the outdoors. He survived a disastrous guided ascent to Mount Everest in 1996, where he and eight other climbers were trapped on the mountain during a storm. Krakauer's pursuits continued to evolve, and he went on to pen the bestselling nonfiction books *Into Thin Air* and *Under the Banner of Heaven*, among others.

Even though this type of fusioneer might not be creating a new domain from scratch, they are combining their passions into something new *for them*. Rather than being forced down a narrow and unsatisfying career path, they can combine their interests and passions into a new, unfolding, and fulfilling pathway.

Expanding a Domain

The second type of fusioneering requires more innovation than the first and involves using knowledge of one or more disciplines to expand another. Contemporary filmmakers such as George Lucas and James Cameron fit into this category. They didn't create a new domain. They are still filmmakers working within an established medium, but they are constantly breaking new ground, redefining what is possible, and expanding the domain. There are many excellent historical examples of this type of fusioneer.

One of thirteen children, Gian Lorenzo Bernini was born in Naples, Italy, in 1598. His father was a sculptor, so he was exposed to art at an early age. In addition to painting, he wrote, directed, and acted in plays. He even designed the sets. Later in life, he worked as an architect and city planner, but in his early twenties, while working under the patronage of Cardinal Scipione Borghese, Bernini first made his mark by sculpting marble masterpieces.

When it came to sculpture, Bernini didn't emulate those who came before him. Instead, he drew inspiration from all forms of art, particularly plays, because he used that understanding of the three-dimensional aspect of the stage and the audience to expand the domain of sculpture. Up to that point, sculptures were more like a fixed column or a cylinder. The Greek and Roman style was stiff and cold. What Bernini did was make sculpture dynamic and three-dimensional. The way he positioned his subjects and used both the foreground and the background to engage the audience in pieces such as *Apollo and Daphne* and *David* broke from convention and changed the way the world viewed sculpture. The way the curves give the impression of fluid motion was influenced by the stage, while the use of darks and lights came from painting.

Expanding an existing domain gives this type of fusioneer space to flourish. They're not limited by the traditions of their field, but by standing on the shoulders of those who came before, they can truly expand that existing domain.

Leading a Fusioneering Team

The third type of fusioneer is a visionary leader, adept in multiple skill sets, who works along with a talented team of people. They may expand an existing domain or create a new one. Many inventors and hands-on entrepreneurs often fall into this category, such as Henry Ford, who created the assembly line, and Tim Berners-Lee, who first launched the World Wide Web. Much like the domain-expanding fusioneer, this type piggybacks on the work, discovery, or expertise of others that came before. They lead or create their own teams, relying upon their contributions to bring reality to their vision. If you look at some of the most significant innovations today, they may not be the work of one person; they are instead helmed by a visionary leader who knows enough about each of the disciplines they are fusing to oversee the process.

Steve Jobs is credited with inventing the iPhone, but a closer look reveals that this historical achievement is much more complicated than the work of any one man. Jobs was the visionary who was the face of the technology and whose name has become synonymous with the iPhone, but he didn't do it alone. On the simplest level, the iPhone fuses the internet with the telephone to create an all-in-one computer we carry around in our pockets. Aside from previous innovations ranging from the touch screen to the lithium battery, there were many collaborative technological breakthroughs during the actual process that made the finished product possible, and they can't all be attributed to Steve Jobs. He had help.

Creating a New Domain Independently

This fourth type is rare, but it can potentially change the world. It's the epitome of self-actualization and one of the quintessential examples of fusioneering: a lone fusioneer creating a new, unique domain.

Born in 1815, Ada Lovelace learned to preoccupy herself as a child by studying math and science. It soon became a passion, and when she married in 1835, her love of mechanics and metaphysics was a significant departure from the typical Victorian wife. "Poetical science" was what she called her analysis, which brought the power of imagination to math and science. Ada's life changed when she met mathematician, engineer, and inventor Charles Babbage, another groundbreaking fusioneer of this type, who created the first mechanical computer, called the Difference Engine. He then improved on that concept to make the Analytical Engine, a more advanced calculator with internal memory and storage. It

Ada Lovelace

was a revolutionary invention but went unappreciated by the average person and the British government, which had bankrolled the project and considered it a failure.

Ada saw this technology very differently from how Babbage did, and she realized its potential went far beyond simply computing numbers. She felt it could ultimately use symbols and math to find order and communicate, maybe even manipulate words and create art or music. So when Ada transcribed Babbage's lectures at the University of Turin from French to English so she could explain the revolutionary benefits of the Analytical Engine to the scientific community, she did so by creating a method for the machine to calculate the Bernoulli number sequence. Today, this is considered the first computer program.

Ada Lovelace never saw her dream come to fruition, but she laid the groundwork for those who made the modern computer a reality. She created a brand-new domain, and she did it on her own. She made connections that nobody had ever made before by combining her knowledge of disciplines. She needed to understand the workings of the mechanical device and the math to create computer programming.

Driven by a unique and consuming vision and an unquenchable curiosity, this type of fusioneer combines multiple passions, interests, and domains into a totally new domain, the outcome of which may very well change the world.

It's important not to feel restricted when considering these four types. This process is inherently fluid, which means there are gray areas and no rigid boundaries. What type of fusioneer you are is not important. One is not better than the others. What's most important is that you have a vision, and you're pursuing that vision. In each case, these fusioneers are pursuing what they love, pushing themselves forward, and finding fulfillment in their work.

FUSE

I chose the path of fusioneering (although I didn't know what to call it at the time) because it allowed me to combine the disciplines I loved—science, robotics, and art—to create something unique while pushing the boundaries of what I was capable of and what was possible. I never could have imagined I'd be where I am today. I'm incredibly fortunate to be able to do what I love. It's the result of many amazing life experiences, but if there are qualities that made it possible for me to reach this point and provide a foundation for fusioneering, they are curiosity, a desire to learn, and pursuing what I loved, all with a vision for moving forward.

Fusioneering is liberating, yet not a completely freewheeling process. Like all the fusioneers mentioned earlier, I didn't have a blueprint to follow. However, when looking back over my journey, I see that there were clearly defined steps. There are no shortcuts, and you can't jump ahead, so I've created the following framework to ensure that you're on the right track. It's only four steps, and it forms a convenient acronym, so it's easy to remember. It's not intended to be restrictive but to help guide you along the way.

Find

The fusioneering process begins with identifying your passions. What inspires you? What lights you up? What do you love to do? And then you combine those passions into a vision for yourself. Being a fusioneer requires following your heart and pursuing what lights a fire in you. This is arguably the most important step, where you discover your inspiration and determine which disciplines you will fuse together. This is about tapping into your passions to form your vision.

Upgrade

You can't be expected to simply start an endeavor like this without preparation. You'll need to improve your current skills, add new skill sets, and become proficient in those as well. This can take time and may require outside resources and input from mentors and experts.

Start

Next is taking action, when you start fusing and begin to make your dream a reality. It won't be easy, but that's part of the joy of learning and improving. No matter how prepared you are, don't expect everything to be perfect. There will be problems and obstacles. During this phase, you may need to continue to develop your vision. It's an ongoing process of exploring, expanding, creating, failing, retrying, and succeeding. The goal is to push the boundaries of what is possible, not get to the finish line.

Fusing science, robotics, and art

Evolve

If Start is about building and creating, Evolve is about growing and expanding, while continuing down the path of your fusioneering journey. A fusioneer can experience this evolution gradually or exponentially. When combining knowledge from multiple domains, it is possible to create unique solutions that someone with expertise in only one discipline might never consider. This opens you up to a whole new world of possibilities.

This framework is designed to be self-motivating, allowing you to pursue your passion with focus and not become overwhelmed or distracted by all the other things you need to do. Most important, it provides room for you to evolve.

Fusioneering is about breaking away from convention to forge your own path. It's a new way to live, structure a career, reach your potential, and achieve self-fulfillment. This alternative pathway isn't reserved just for the unsatisfied. Those who benefit can include young people venturing out into the world, those curious individuals in search of something more meaningful, the happy professionals open to a new possibility, or anyone—young or old—with interests in multiple disciplines who wants more creativity in their life. Fusioneering allows you to restructure the ways you think about the world and creates new possibilities.

Fusing art and science

INTING
YALE
George Braziller
the Ground Up
A K PETERS
tational Geometry
3rd Edition
and
pment
Dunn & Parberry
e Art of Painting Softly
THE CLARK
EDITED BY DAVID BLAYNEY BROWN,
AMY CONCANNON AND SAM SMILES
TATE
Turner
Gerh
MARTIN K

PART 1

FIND

Your journey begins by identifying the passions and the activities that light you up inside. Once you can better recognize those things that make you tick, you can then creatively combine them—fuse them together—to create your vision. This is the first and most important part of the fusioneering process. At this point, you should feel excitement, but this can also come with uncertainty and apprehension. This is why you need to do your homework and thoroughly investigate the feasibility of what you want to do.

What inspires you? What imagined future version of yourself excites you? If you love travel and you're a good writer, you put those two together in a way that feels natural to you. That might be becoming a travel writer or a marketing copywriter for far-off hotels. But it goes well beyond a job description. Being a fusioneer isn't just about combining what you're good at. It's about uncovering your unique gifts and passions, finding what your whole being says you should be doing, and then leading an unfolding, fulfilling life. That's your fusioneering vision.

Once you've formulated your fusioneering vision, it will provide you with an endless source of energy while helping you overcome challenges and obstacles on your journey. It's perfectly fine if you don't yet have your vision, but you should begin thinking about it early. That discovery will better prepare you to recognize all the possibilities that come with it, and you never know when inspiration might strike.

Willis Carrier was an electrical engineer working for a heating and ventilation company in 1902. One of the buildings his company oversaw was home to a publishing firm that experienced problems one muggy morning. The heat and humidity made the paper swell and shrink, so the colors didn't align on the pages when they went through the printing press. Temperature control was possible at the time but not humidity control. Carrier was tasked with finding a way to make the air inside the building less humid without making it too dry, but he was stumped. Weeks later, Carrier was standing on a train platform on a foggy day when he discovered his solution. He knew fog was air that was one hundred percent saturated with water, so what if he used that as a starting point and then added dry air to reduce humidity to fifty-five percent? He would recreate fog and then use water to remove moisture from the air. It worked, and that device used to control humidity became what we know today as the air conditioner. The problem Carrier faced gave him a purpose. Although he didn't know how at that time, he had a vision to solve it. Fortunately, being open to new ideas, he seized the moment when inspiration struck on that train platform.

I've experienced three epiphanies in my life that have shaped my fusioneering journey, so I think a lot about inspiration and where it comes from. There are many theories out there, and people have written entire books on the subject, but I've found that attempts to dramatize and dissect the nature of inspiration often feel forced. It's putting constraints on an organic process. One reason is that inspiration is difficult to define. It means different things to different people and can come in many forms, but almost everyone agrees that you can't force inspiration. Just as you can't surprise yourself with a present or purposefully scare yourself when looking in the mirror, you aren't in control of your inspiration. Does that mean inspiration is a gift that is bestowed upon us? In a way, aren't all of our talents, interests, and good fortune gifts that we should recognize and embrace?

One common interpretation of inspiration I disagree with is that it's a bolt out of the blue that delivers a fully formed vision, a pathway to your fusioneer self. Instead, I view inspiration as a moment of insight, a spark. It's not a fire yet, just that initial spark that has the potential to burn long and bright. On its own, it's useless, but if cared for over time, kept fueled by constant poking and prodding, it can become the brightly burning fire that is your fully formed vision.

While I believe that everyone is capable of experiencing inspiration, not everyone is open or prepared to receive it. Nobody has a monopoly on good ideas, and while you can't control when inspiration might strike, you can create optimal conditions that allow you to identify and nurture inspiration when it arrives. That's the purpose behind the exercises in this section. I've included assessments that have helped me along the way and designed new ones specifically for this process, so you can see things from a new perspective. While I can't give you the answers, I can tell stories and ask questions that will help you figure out those answers for yourself, which may lead to the formulation of your vision.

You might know the passions and interests you want to fuse and have already created your vision for going forward. If so, you're ahead of the game, but it wouldn't hurt to go through the assessments and do the exercises. Some results might seem obvious and tell you what you already know, while others might change your perspective and help you look at your life in a new light. Use what works, and disregard what doesn't.

Your vision will be stronger and self-sustaining if it is directly connected to your purpose. Purpose means different things to different people, and people often have different names for it, but my favorite interpretation comes from Stephen Cope, who, in his book *The Great Work of Your Life*, refers to it as dharma, or sacred duty. Call it whatever you want; that purpose will be unique to you. It doesn't need to make sense to anyone else. Once incorporated into your vision, it will become a vital energy source that will empower you throughout your journey. Along the way, if ever you feel unsure, your purpose will be your guide.

To formulate your vision and purpose in life, you must first better understand yourself. This will allow you to find your vision, inspiration, and purpose. Next, you'll need to identify the passions you'll fuse together.

With self-reflection and by identifying those passions, along with perhaps some helpful inspirations, you can formulate a vision that is truly yours. If it is underlined by your true purpose—your reason for being—it will be all the stronger for you as your life unfolds, helping you to achieve fulfillment, as you were meant to.

When you discover your fusioneering vision, you may feel hesitation: "Is that truly what I want to do?" Then you'll have an indescribable excitement, along with natural trepidation, but you'll know. It will just feel right.

CHAPTER 1

This Is Who I Am

She may no longer be a household name, and few people today have even seen movies such as *Samson and Delilah*, *Algiers*, and *The Strange Woman*, but back in the 1940s, Hedy Lamarr was one of Hollywood's biggest stars and was considered one of the most beautiful women in the world. However, she wasn't only an actress but also a fusioneer and inventor who helped create the technology that would later be the basis for WiFi, Bluetooth, and GPS.

Born in Austria in 1914, Lamarr's earliest inspiration came from her father. He was a local bank director but was fascinated with how machines worked. Together, they often took apart and reassembled the various trinkets around the house. When she became a teenager, she was drawn to the stage and gained notoriety as a European art-house actress. One of her biggest fans was an Austrian arms dealer, Fritz Mandl. When they married in 1933, Lamarr's life took a turn for the worse. Her new husband forbade her from acting, and she began to feel like a prisoner in her marriage. The Jewish Lamarr was often forced to mingle with her husband's Nazi associates, whom they frequently entertained at their home.

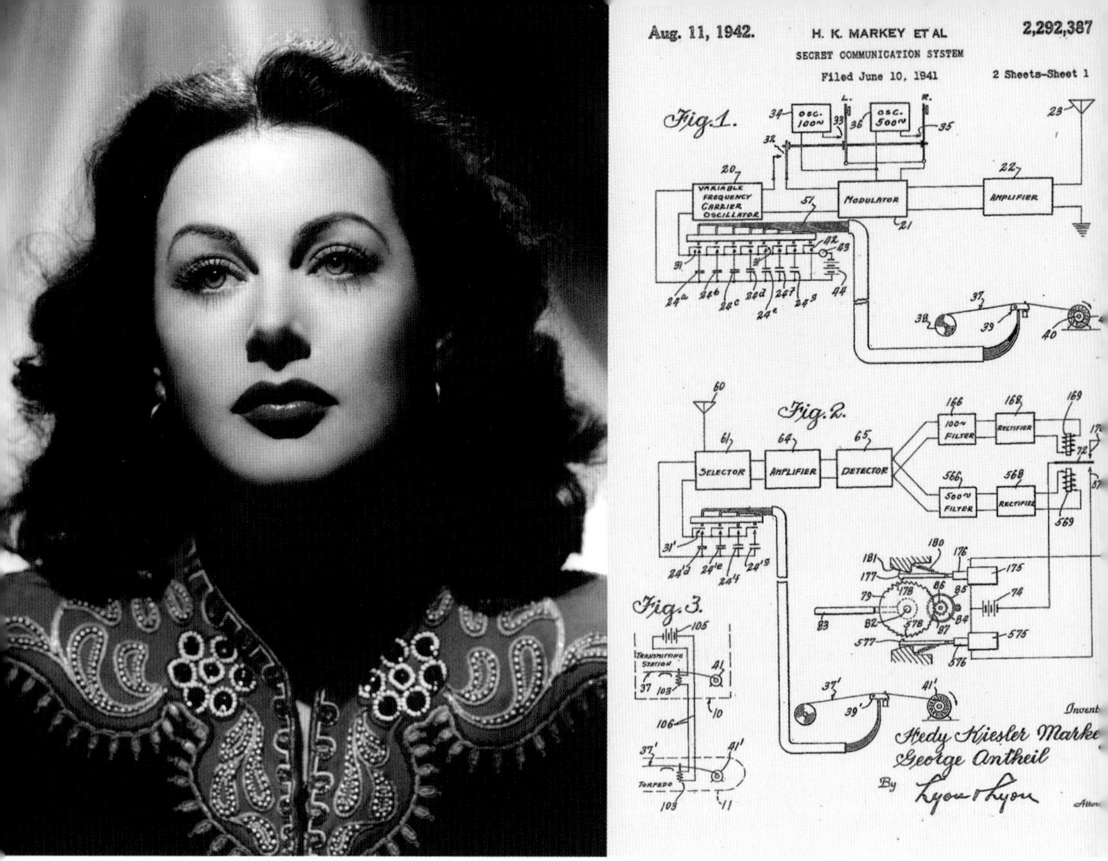

Hedy Lamarr with her US patent

In 1937, Lamarr escaped her husband and Austria by fleeing to London. A chance meeting with MGM studio head Louis B. Mayer helped launch what turned out to be a promising Hollywood movie career. She starred opposite such big names as James Stewart, Clark Gable, and Spencer Tracy, but her work off camera was even more fascinating.

After achieving fame and fortune through acting, Lamarr remained curious about the world and how it worked. Once in Hollywood, she dated the American business magnate Howard Hughes. He gave her a behind-the-scenes look at his factories and even provided her with electronic equipment that she set up in her home and movie trailer to tinker with during her spare time. When Hughes hit a speed bump in his attempt to design the world's fastest airplane, Lamarr helped provide the breakthrough. At the time, all wing designs were straight across and perpendicular to the fuselage. After studying the movements of birds and fish, Lamarr suggested angling the plane wings backward to better emulate a bird's wing and a fish's fin. Upon hearing this suggestion, Hughes called her a genius.

Inventing things came naturally to Lamarr. She upgraded a stoplight and created a tablet that dissolved in water to make a Coke-like carbonated beverage. And she did it all while working as a Hollywood actress. But during World War II, she used fusioneering to do her most ambitious and impressive work.

Lamarr wanted to serve her country. She was uncomfortable making so much money as an actress while her homeland was being torn apart and the Jewish people were being sent to camps. Most Hollywood stars used their celebrity to sell war bonds to the public, but Lamarr wanted to do more, and ironically, her failed marriage to an Austrian arms dealer gave her the idea of how to help.

Early during the war, German U-boats were wreaking havoc in the Atlantic. The Allied ships struggled to defend themselves because the enemy could easily jam the Allied-guided torpedo signals. That's when Lamarr saw an opportunity to use her innovative talents. Her idea was to create an intricate, jam-proof, radio-controlled guidance system by continually sequencing through random frequencies. She sought the help of avant-garde composer George Antheil because she felt the system could be controlled like the automated piano keys in Antheil's work. The design resembled an old perforated player piano roll. The torpedo transmitter and the receiver were synchronized and had identical tapes, with similar perforations for frequency hopping. The signal could hop among eighty-eight frequencies—the same number as keys on a piano. Since the Nazi jammers could only block a single frequency at a time, Lamarr and Antheil's invention would make it virtually impossible for the enemy to jam the Allied communications.

Lamarr and Antheil were awarded a patent in 1942, but the US government didn't take the musician and actress seriously. Because of her Austrian descent, some feared that Lamarr might even be a spy, so the Navy didn't utilize this invention until the 1960s. However, frequency-hopping technology later became the basis for spread spectrum—spreading the transmitted signal across a spectrum of frequencies—and was incorporated into the WiFi, Bluetooth, and GPS technology we're familiar with today.

Hedy Lamarr struggled for most of her life to be seen as anything more than an actress and a pretty face. She didn't receive the credit she deserved for her innovation until much later in life. She lived her final years out of the public eye, but an inspiring audiotape she left for her son proved that she didn't have any regrets. She said, "Give the world the best you have, and you will be kicked in the teeth. Give the world the best you got anyway." In other words, don't give up when faced with challenges.

The story of Hedy Lamarr is an excellent and unlikely example of fusioneering. Without any formal training, she fused music, motors, radio frequencies, transmitters and receivers, electromechanical control, circuitry, and math. Her story also demonstrates how doing what comes naturally plays a crucial role in our vision. While Lamarr might have been introduced to the world of weaponry when married to her arms dealer ex-husband, it was her curiosity that led to her amazing invention and the creation of concepts that are still used today. She used her imagination, skills, and what came most naturally to expand the domain of military defense by creating something entirely new. Like Hedy Lamarr, we all have inherent talents and skills. Fusioneering is about recognizing and embracing those as you set out on your journey.

What Comes Naturally

While working with brain-damaged patients, Harvard psychologist and researcher Howard Gardner learned that injuries to different parts of the brain would influence what these patients could and couldn't do. Some would lose language skills, while others lost spatial awareness. He recognized these same disparities when working with kids. Some were good at math, others at language, and others at music. Kids had different talents, yet math and language skills were primarily what determined intelligence. Those skills were the basis for IQ tests and often determined how well one would do in school, but just because a kid didn't have math and language skills didn't mean they weren't intelligent. There wasn't only one way to be smart.

That concept was the basis for Gardner's 1983 book, *Frames of Mind*, in which he took a pluralistic view of intelligence and broadened the definition to include seven different types. He has since expanded this to nine types that reflect how one learns, processes data, and interacts with the world. They include linguistic, logical–mathematical, bodily–kinesthetic, spatial–visual, musical, interpersonal, intrapersonal, naturalist, and existential frames of mind.

The linguistic frame of mind involves language, reading, speaking, and writing. Picture someone who loves to tell stories or spends their time doing crossword puzzles. It involves a fundamental understanding of the meaning of words and how to string them together in writing and speech. This intelligence carries over well to traditional schooling.

Those with a logical–mathematical frame of mind naturally recognize numerical and logical patterns and categories. Aside from an interest in math and science, people who enjoy strategizing and experimenting also fit into this category. It involves critical thinking and organization to help solve abstract problems. It's the type of intelligence that carries over well to IQ and standardized tests.

A bodily–kinesthetic frame of mind is physical intelligence. It's common in athletes, actors, dancers, and those drawn to physical activity but also those who are good with their hands and certain crafts like sewing and woodworking. These are people who can handle their bodies and other objects skillfully.

People with spatial–visual intelligence think in terms of images and pictures. They can think abstractly, are good at puzzles and mazes, and can build things because they can recognize and manipulate patterns. Artists and those who can judge distances and accurately read a map also fit into this category. It's an intelligence that can help architects, engineers, chess players, and surgeons.

Some people have an ear for music, for rhythm, pitch, tone, and timbre. Others don't, but musical intelligence goes beyond playing and composing music to include those who listen and pay attention to sounds in their environment that others might easily miss. That might include bird-watchers and ornithologists, who identify species by their calls.

An interpersonal frame of mind is the first of two intelligences that deal directly with human beings. Not only does this category include those who get along with people and who communicate well but also those who are leaders. It often comes down to understanding the feelings, moods, emotions, and motives of others, which helps those with this intelligence work well with people. Actors, politicians, and salespeople can fit into this category.

Intrapersonal intelligence also deals with human beings, specifically self-awareness. This is not a skill everyone possesses, but this intelligence is about more than being aware of how you feel. It also involves being self-reliant, self-motivated, and in tune with your values, fears, and beliefs. It includes controlling your thoughts and accurately understanding your strengths and weaknesses. Leaders naturally fall into this category.

The naturalist frame of mind was added by Gardner after coming up with the original seven. It's the ability to feel at home outdoors. Those who like hunting, fishing, hiking, camping, and nature have natural intelligence. Biologists and farmers fit into this category.

Those with existential intelligence are comfortable tackling deep questions about existence, love, and even the nature of life.

Spirituality and theology also fit into this category, because they involve being curious and trying to understand our place in the world. It's an intelligence that almost every young kid has but doesn't always nurture.

Since linguistic and logical intelligence are given the most focus in school, other forms of intelligence could be neglected. That can lead some kids to be labeled underachievers because they don't fit into the traditional box. This can also carry over into the workforce. If people aren't able to tap into their natural intelligences, they might find themselves doing work that doesn't come easily or match their strengths.

Looking over this list of nine intelligences can be quite revealing for yourself. Which ones do you think best describe you? What comes naturally to you? What are your strengths? Do those align with how you make a living and spend your time? Asking yourself these questions is a good place to start self-reflection and honing your vision. However, this list shouldn't be your only consideration, because it won't paint a complete picture. Just because you're good at something doesn't mean you enjoy it or are comfortable doing it.

What You Love

Andre Agassi is listed among the top ten all-time earners in professional tennis. During his twenty-year career, he was ranked number one in the world and won eight majors, sixty tournament titles, and an Olympic gold medal. He started playing at three, and people could recognize his talent at five. He turned professional at sixteen and dedicated his life to the sport, but in his 2009 bestselling memoir, *Open*, he famously said, "I play tennis for a living, even though I hate tennis, hate it with a dark and secret passion, and always have."

In that book, Agassi talks about being groomed by his overbearing father to become a tennis superstar from the time he could walk. He was a great player, but this pursuit of being the best consumed his life and caused him to hate the sport. The pressure and stress took their toll on his body and mind, leading to depression and drug abuse. He admits that some of his worst moments occurred when he was ranked number one in the world. Why did he keep playing? Tennis was all he knew, and he was one of the best tennis players in the world. If he didn't play, what else would he do?

Agassi eventually came to terms with his fate and realized that even though he didn't choose his life, he still had to take ownership of it. He realized that other kids had far less opportunity and choice than he did, and he wanted to do something about it. He refers to that as his epiphany but admits, "Epiphanies don't change your life. It's what you do with them that changes your life." That's when he began his philanthropic work and found his true calling in helping disadvantaged youths. Finding your own true calling is a crucial part of being a fusioneer.

It's easy to see how athletes, actors, and anyone who lives in the public eye can become disillusioned with their path in life, but this phenomenon isn't reserved for the famous. No matter how talented you are at something, pressures and responsibilities can cause you to sour on what you're good at. You can be a tremendous call center rep with a unique gift to get irate customers to calm down, but you go home drained and miserable every night. You can be a great restaurant server but hate working with people. You can be a strong accountant but find the work dull.

The more you think about it, you can probably find many things you're good at but don't particularly love to do, and no vision can be complete without considering what you love. You want this pursuit to be fun and exciting. You want to feel like you are being propelled forward on your fusioneering journey, not forcing yourself to do the work. That starts by incorporating what you love into your vision.

John W. Weeks Memorial Bridge crossing the Charles River

Your Passions

The vision for my fusioneering journey was formulated while I attended the Harvard Business School. It happened on Sunday, October 23, 1977, at 5:50 p.m. I was crossing a footbridge over the Charles River on my way to six o'clock mass at the Church of Saint Paul, just off Harvard Square. I was thinking about the results of a self-assessment quiz I had recently taken. After answering a hundred multiple-choice questions, we were given a graph that displayed our score in the following six categories: political, social, religious, economic, aesthetic, and theoretical. The idea was to show our level of interest in each area, not our respective aptitudes. While political, social, and economic were lower on the graph, I showed a strong interest in the aesthetic and an even stronger interest in the theoretical. That mirrored what I loved doing.

Standing right there on that footbridge, I thought, *What if I combine them?* I was struck with this idea of fusing the aesthetic with the theoretical—art and science.

I hurried to make it to the service on time, and once I arrived, my mind raced. I struggled to sit still and squirmed throughout mass. Once the service was over, I rushed around the corner to Elsie's, a local sandwich shop. There wasn't any paper, so I grabbed a paper plate and wrote down my thoughts on the back. I had so much energy and excitement when describing my vision on that plate that I can almost feel it today. It's something I will never forget, and that paper plate is now framed on the wall in my studio.

While this idea may seem like it was a bolt out of the blue, it directly resulted from my lived experience. I was in my second year at HBS and was enrolled in an elective called Self-Assessment and Career Development. The year before, it had won the Exxon award for the country's best new innovative business school class. We had to write one paper in the first half of the semester and another in the second half. There was no exam, which was unusual for HBS. Our entire grade was based on those two papers. I wrote the first about my tech background: working for HP Labs, being an engineer, and my Air Force experience. When it came time to write the second paper about developing a career plan, I struggled to come up with an idea suited for a business school student, especially given my self-assessment results. That's what I was trying to figure out while crossing that footbridge.

The idea to combine art and science is what I refer to as my first epiphany. I call it an epiphany because it was so much more than inspiration. It was a special and profound realization that changed the course of my life. It had a significant impact, yet the idea had been so simple, and it was right in front of me. I just never thought about it in those terms before. It took looking at things from a different perspective and closely analyzing what I loved to truly see it. Looking at my interests quantified on those test results was enough to create a spark and give me the idea to combine them. Had I not taken that self-assessment class, I might never have experienced that epiphany.

Many of the assessment exercises from that class and those readily available online aren't well suited for a book like this. We don't have the benefit of inputting answers and having an algorithm spit out results. However, a self-assessment isn't necessary to get in touch with your passion and understand what lights you up. Sometimes, all you need to do is write about your thoughts and experiences.

That was the basis for one of my most memorable self-assessments at HBS. There are different versions of this, but it's often referred to as the Seven Stories, and it was based on the work of author Bernard Haldane, who is sometimes referred to as the father of career development. He used this assessment to help military veterans find their calling after serving in World War II.

If you've taken a career development class before, you might be familiar with this exercise, but I've modified it slightly for fusioneering. This is the type of exercise where you get out what you put in. Remember that nobody will ever read this but you, so it's in your best interest to be honest. Approach it with an open mind, and the results might surprise you. Take your time, and go at your own pace.

Step 1: Your Experiences and Accomplishments

Write down at least twenty accomplishments or experiences that you enjoyed or that gave you satisfaction. No need to elaborate or go into detail yet. This is more of a brainstorming exercise. Your answers can range from landing a job to putting together a model train set in your spare time. These answers don't need to be in any order or be things anybody else knows about. It might help if you start earlier in life and progress forward while recalling other examples. This list will be unique to you. Don't feel like you have to do this in one sitting. Take as much time as needed. The more you think about it, the more items you will recall, and the more accurate your list will become. Don't move on until you have completed your list.

Step 2: Narrowing Down Your List

Once you have your list of at least twenty accomplishments, you can begin ranking them. The idea is to winnow this list down to the seven distinct experiences that are the most significant to you. If you get stuck or find it difficult to put these experiences in order, try ranking them by the level of enjoyment.

Step 3: Write Your Stories

Write a story for each of these seven experiences. Go into detail and be as descriptive as possible. Try to identify what made these particular experiences stand out. Here are some questions that can help your thinking. Not all will apply, so try answering the ones that do.

- What did you enjoy most about this experience?
- What was your motivation?
- What made you proud?
- Was anybody else involved?
- What was the reason for your success?
- What skills did this accomplishment require?
- Did the result surprise you?
- How did this experience make you feel?

Don't treat this like homework or be constrained by word count. Free associate and ramble if that's what feels natural. The goal is to articulate the experience and explain why it resonated with you as accurately as possible.

Step 4: Look for Patterns

Once you finish writing all seven stories, take some time before returning to what you wrote. You want to have a fresh set of eyes when you read over these stories. The goal of this exercise is to look for patterns in what you love to do and excel at. Look closely at the words you used to describe each of these accomplishments. Look specifically for *action verbs*. I encourage you to review all your pages, print them out, and then highlight all of the action verbs in yellow. It's easy to do and so revealing.

When I did this exercise back in 1977, I saw that I kept using the words *build*, *create*, and *design* over and over again. That's what I enjoyed doing more than anything else, so it made sense that those actions were at the core of what I felt were my greatest joys and accomplishments. It was true then, and it remains true today.

Now, look back over those action words that stand out in your stories and ask yourself the following questions:

- Which actions (or verbs) are repeated most often?
- What do those actions say about where my interests lie?
- How often in my current work or personal life do I follow these desires?
- Do I fully embrace what lights me up, or has it been stifled or neglected?
- How can I incorporate these actions into my fusioneering vision?

This exercise isn't about values; it's about developing self-awareness, understanding what drives you, and then seeing how well that lines up in your daily life. Sometimes, it merely takes looking at your life from a slightly different perspective to truly see it. As it was for me, this exercise might be the single best way to gain insight about yourself.

Your Reason for Being

Tapping into your passion to do what you love is one of the most important criteria when honing your vision. Even more important than discovering your passion is understanding your purpose, your dharmic responsibility in life. If passion is what you love to do, purpose is what you're supposed to be doing.

I was recently introduced to the Japanese concept of *ikigai*, which translates to "reason for being." Living one's *ikigai* often provides a feeling of accomplishment and fulfillment because it allows you to live in a more natural way and be in tune with what you are supposed to be doing in life. It helps bring meaning to life and has been linked to longevity and happiness. Business coach Marc Winn has redefined *ikigai* to mean where passion, mission, vocation, and profession overlap. He created the following Venn diagram, which you might already be familiar with.

To apply Winn's version of the *ikigai* model for yourself, you must start by asking yourself the following four questions:

1. What are you good at?
2. What do you love?
3. What does the world need?
4. What can you get paid for?

For each question in this brainstorming exercise, think of as many answers as possible. If you've been following along with the previous exercises, you've already done most of the heavy lifting. You have started to better understand and appreciate your interests, skills, passions, and accomplishments. This concept of *ikigai* will take you a valuable and insightful step further because no one question outweighs another. What's important to consider is where your answers overlap. If you have the same answer for all four questions, that is considered your *ikigai*, your reason for being. However, that is not the only way to look at this exercise.

Ikigai Venn diagram

Notice how the original four circles overlap in four additional areas. I'll call these *wings* for our purposes. You can extrapolate a lot about yourself by studying your wings. Here is the simple way this breaks down.

- Passion: An overlap of what you love and what you're good at
- Mission: An overlap of what the world needs and what you love
- Profession: An overlap of what you're good at and what you can be paid for
- Vocation: An overlap of what the world needs and what you can be paid for

All of these exercises were designed to help you identify your purpose. Whether you call it your *ikigai*, your reason for being, your dharmic responsibility, or simply what you should be doing with your life, it will play a crucial role in creating your vision. Nothing says your purpose must be part of your vision; you are free to fuse whatever interests and passions you want. However, your vision will be more meaningful to you if it's connected to your purpose. Knowing your purpose will provide a continual source of energy on your visionary journey. If you happen to get lost along the way or feel adrift, reconnecting with your purpose can bring you back to your path. Think of it as your compass or North Star.

Some people already live life aligned with their passions, strengths, and interests, so their answers might seem obvious. For others, life has taken them away from their true nature or pushed them toward specialization without realizing it. Whether through pressure to earn a living, make money, or achieve status, it's easy to convince ourselves that we are doing what's prudent, only to feel unfulfilled years later and not understand why. If you've experienced that, you might have drifted from your passions and purpose, so try to identify any passions that you might have turned your back on.

Before moving on, review with fresh eyes what you've learned about yourself in the Seven Stories exercise and the insights you gained with the *ikigai* exercise. Are there any patterns? Can you spot any themes? Our goal here is to compile a thoughtful list of your interests and passions to provide insights into your purpose in life. With that list complete, you now have the opportunity to fuse these interests and passions into an exciting, personal vision for yourself going forward.

CHAPTER 2

Fusing Your Passions

Our educational system and society steer us toward specialization. While that might be the best path for some, it forces others to turn their backs on their passions and interests, which can leave them feeling disillusioned or unfulfilled. Fusioneering doesn't force you to make that choice. You can fuse those interests, activities, and passions into a purposeful vision. How you go about doing that will depend on your vision and your circumstances. What follows are the stories of three fusioneers who each found a different way to successfully navigate this part of the process.

Sarah

Both of Sarah's parents were accountants. She was good at math as a kid, so it was natural that she too become an accountant. Right out of college, she landed a position with a respectable firm in Seattle and worked her way up the ranks over the years. She didn't hate her job. She was good at it, and she made good money. There wasn't anything else she was dying to do, and she didn't see many other options, given her expertise, so she set out to become the best accountant possible. She was single and enjoyed living on her own in Seattle, but something was missing. She just couldn't pinpoint what it was.

When Sarah attended a friend's wedding on a working ranch in northern Montana, everything changed. The ranch was huge—twenty thousand acres. It wasn't only a luxury dude ranch. They bred horses, and it was a destination for many famous guests who used to go there on the hush-hush. Princess Diana even brought her sons there back in the 1990s.

Sarah used to ride horses as a kid and, for a short while, even considered becoming a vet, but it didn't seem like a practical option, so she put her head down and focused on what she thought she was best at. So when she arrived at the ranch for the wedding, she immediately fell in love. She realized how much she missed nature, the outdoors, and being around animals. A part of her didn't want to return home to the city. That's when she realized what was missing from her life and career in Seattle. Because of that experience on the ranch, she was reconnected with a passion she had abandoned as a child.

During the wedding reception, Sarah met a woman who was a traveling veterinarian for the ranchers. She owned her own truck and would travel from ranch to ranch providing her mobile services. She was even on call for certain ranches that she could quickly respond to during an emergency. That's when Sarah had her epiphany. *What if I go from ranch to ranch as an accountant, just like the vet?* Those Montana ranches were a big business, and it seemed like there was an opportunity there. Making a living was part of her criteria, but only one part. She discovered a way to fuse her interests so she could make a living while also doing something she loved, and that allowed her to reconnect with the childhood passion she had turned her back on. That was her vision.

Tom

Tom was a married father of two girls, fourteen and eleven. He grew up in a quiet Colorado suburb with a big family who loved the outdoors. He was constantly going on camping and fishing trips as a kid. He was also a good student who had a gift for numbers. Math came naturally to him, and after college, he started working as a data scientist for a software company in downtown Denver. He never left.

Tom wasn't unhappy. His family life was good, and he earned good money, but work was becoming draining. He found himself dreading going into the office on some days. Once he had kids, he and his wife did not go on as many camping and fishing trips as they used to. Still, he made sure to get away a few times a year and increasingly looked forward to those trips with family and close friends. He sometimes thought about switching careers, but his job was stable, and with the thought of having to pay college tuition for two girls, he didn't think he had the luxury to start over. Even if he did, what would he even do? He had only worked in this one field his entire career. Like many, Tom felt stuck, and although his job wasn't unbearable yet, he worried about its impact on his mental health and happiness in ten or twenty years.

Tom sat down and completed the Seven Stories exercise. At first, it felt automatic. He could easily rattle off the major accomplishments of his life. He didn't need the exercise to tell him he enjoyed fishing, hiking, and birding. He had been doing that since he was a kid, and those were the activities he looked forward to. What made this exercise so effective was that Tom took some extra time and dove deeper to see what he could come up with beyond the obvious answers. That required digging into his past and looking at some of the less obvious accomplishments and enjoyments he experienced throughout his life.

During spring break when in college, Tom took a trip to Paris with his girlfriend. They saw all the sights and made all the required tourist stops. The one that made the biggest impression was the Louvre, specifically the entrance designed by I. M. Pei. Back home, Tom was enrolled in an introduction to architecture class that he randomly selected when he needed to come up with an extra elective. He was surprised that he enjoyed the class as much as he did. They had recently discussed the work of I. M. Pei. Seeing pictures of the Louvre online was one thing but experiencing it in person created a much more powerful response that piqued his curiosity.

When Tom returned from Paris and resumed class, he took a deeper interest in the material. It became his favorite class by far. There were many works and individual pieces that he appreciated, but it was Frank Lloyd Wright's Fallingwater that resonated with him the most. Tom did well in that class, but when the semester ended, he turned his attention back to his major.

Tom was reminded of his earlier interest in architecture when doing the Seven Stories and *ikigai* exercises. After analyzing which type of intelligence fit him best, he knew he had *natural* and *logical-mathematical* intelligence. He also had a keen *spatial-visual* intelligence, which was why architecture had made such an impact on him in college. He had never made that connection before, but looking back on his experience with fresh eyes, he could see it from a different perspective. And a piece like Fallingwater, with cascading water nestled among trees, appealed to all three intelligences. His connections to nature, math, and architecture now seemed obvious.

Tom loved nature, and it had been a major part of his life as a child, but he never considered it a career option. He was good at math, so when he got older, it never occurred to him that he should look beyond that. Now, his mind raced with new ideas for fusing his passions, and his vision underwent multiple iterations. What appealed most to him was the idea of becoming a landscape architect. That was the perfect fusion of his passions, talents, and intelligences.

Noah

Noah had recently graduated college with a degree in English literature. It wasn't an easy road for him. His grades were low in high school, so he had to attend community college before being accepted to a four-year school. He also needed to work his way through college, so he found a job as a server at a local restaurant and waited tables four nights a week. He was already receiving financial aid, so he earned enough money to get by and was also able to save a little extra. He was constantly busy but thrived and enjoyed it. He loved it so much that he dreaded graduation because he didn't yet know what he wanted to do with his life.

Most of Noah's friends were anxious to graduate so they could start making money. They had their sights set on working creative jobs in marketing or getting their foot in the door at a startup, but that didn't interest him at all. He couldn't picture himself working in an office. During his final year of college, he developed a love of writing, but he didn't view that as a realistic career option. Becoming a professional writer seemed like such a long shot, and he didn't even know where to begin looking for a job. He felt unqualified for many of the freelance writing positions that were advertised on job boards, and they paid so little money that he wouldn't be able to support himself after school. However, writing wasn't his only interest.

More than anything else, Noah wanted to get out and see the world before settling down and deciding on a career. As a child, he watched a documentary on the Amazonian rainforest and fell in love with the area. He watched that documentary dozens of times and was drawn to videos and articles about the wildlife and cultures of South America. As he grew older, he dreamed of traveling to Brazil so he could view the country for himself and meet the people, but it was more of a pipe dream, something he would do for fun later in life when he was settled down and had the means to travel the world.

After college graduation, Noah still wasn't any closer to knowing what he wanted to do with his life. He knew that he needed to make some extra money first, so he kept working at the restaurant. However, his eyes were opened when he took the Seven Story and *ikigai* assessments. While he was very much in tune with what he loved and where his talent lay, he had never thought it possible to fuse his passions. The dream to get out and see the world still burned inside him. He enjoyed writing, and he learned in school that he was good at it. That's when he experienced an *aha!* moment. The solution to his problem of what to do after college had been right in front of him, but he never saw it because he didn't think it was possible to fuse his interests. Now he had a plan: He would combine his love of writing with his desire to travel to become a travel writer.

How to Put It All Together

Think of your vision as the seat of a stool, and the legs of the stool as the domains of knowledge you need to support that vision. Your stool may have two legs, four legs, six legs, or more. It all depends on your vision and the domains required to support and bring that vision to life.

If you don't yet know the domains you want to fuse, don't worry. The following exercises will stimulate your imagination for what might be possible.

Mix and Match Brainstorming

Try turning this process into a series of creative journal exercises. Start by pairing up your list of passions and activities. Create two identical vertical columns, and then list every possible pairing. If you have five passions and activities, that's ten pairings to explore. The possibilities associated with some pairings might not seem obvious at first or might not even make sense, but take the time to brainstorm and freely jot down some ideas for each. No one else will ever read what you write, so there is no need to be self-conscious. Give yourself the freedom to write whatever associations you can imagine. You might be surprised by the result.

Utilize Technology

If you want more ideas, use resources such as Google and ChatGPT to help you brainstorm ways to fuse your passions and activities. While you can't rely on technology to create a fully formed vision on your behalf, it's a great way to open your eyes to possibilities that you might not think of on your own. Noah found these resources especially helpful, and they jump-started his research into topics and themes for future travel articles.

Let Your Purpose Be Your Guide

Some people might struggle to formulate a single vision. Others might have the opposite problem and be torn between two or more visions. If you're having trouble, refer back to your *ikigai*, and ask yourself what vision best allows you to live in alignment with your reason for being. This is the vision that will be more natural for you to pursue, and in the long term, it will provide the most fulfillment.

Purpose serves as an excellent filter. It will often lead to the path of least internal resistance and the path you enjoy most. It also prevents you from pursuing a vision for the wrong reasons. Hedy Lamarr's vision was to help the war effort. Her purpose was to improve the torpedo guidance system and protect it from jamming. My vision was to combine art and science. My purpose was to build a robot that could create large, impressive paintings. Your purpose is how you express your vision, and once you've formulated that vision, it's time to investigate its feasibility.

CHAPTER 3

Is Your Dream Realistic?

I can say without a doubt that Harvard Business School was the hardest thing I've ever done, much more challenging than military basic training. It was so intense that I barely had time to go to the bathroom for the first two weeks. There were five classes a semester—three a day—and after each class, we'd get three new case studies for each class the following day. Each case study focused on an actual company. They were roughly fifteen to twenty-five pages long and included information about a company, along with some of its financials. Each case presented a difficult situation or problem the company faced, be it marketing, competition, finance, manufacturing, HR, international business, or any combination. We had to step into the role of CEO and figure out what to do.

After discussing a thousand cases over two years, we learned how to think like a CEO when faced with complex situations. Harvard taught me the difference between knowledge (studying to retain information) and wisdom (insight and understanding). In other words, what I learned at Harvard Business School was the ability to think.

I was one of the few students with an engineering background. Manufacturing and production classes came naturally to me. I liked building things with my hands, and since I had been so immersed in learning all about the business world, my first epiphany that I wrote down on that paper plate in Elsie's sandwich shop involved creating a business—a manufacturing company, to be specific. I wanted to use my experience working with microprocessors and programmable memory to build a robot that could turn pictures into paintings. It was a natural way to combine what I was good at (the scientific, technical, and aesthetic) while also making money by running a business. People would send in their orders, and the robot would recreate their picture as a painting. I'd set up a warehouse and turn it into a factory, where I created and shipped paintings. However, the idea would have to wait. I first needed to make a living and pay off my student loans.

When I graduated from Harvard in 1978, microprocessors were relatively new, and there was so much exciting promise surrounding the new technology. Having already worked at Hewlett-Packard's corporate research labs in Palo Alto, it was natural that I wanted to return to HP—specifically, the division introducing its new, proprietary, high-performance processor. This was the same time frame when Steve Jobs and Bill Gates were also independently working with microprocessors. I also wanted to return to Colorado, where I had lived during my four years in the Air Force. I had other job opportunities, but none were as appealing as the one offered by Pat Welch, the head of marketing for the division at HP that would incorporate the microprocessor into new computer products.

When I worked in the Air Force research lab, I was on the technical side, but I would now be a product manager in charge of a marketing team. One of our jobs was to introduce HP's newest and fastest computer, which also had the first-ever color display in the

Paul's design and handiwork: soldering control circuits for his first robot, 1980-1981

company's history. We did some great cutting-edge work, and my career was going well, but I never forgot about that first epiphany to fuse art and science.

In 1981, I developed some initial ideas for a business plan, while I started building the robot. On the weekends, I'd take home a new computer from HP (which retailed for $50,000 back then) to run my prototype robot. Since I was the product manager, I wasn't breaking any rules. The equipment manager helped me load it into my car on Fridays after work. It was fun. Just like when I was a kid playing with my Erector set, I wanted to see what I could build.

I knew there was a lot I needed to learn to make my vision a reality. That's why I took a machine shop class at the vo-tech center. I then bought a milling machine and set up a small machine shop in my garage. I assembled the motors and gearing, soldered circuit boards, hooked the robot up to the computer, and then wrote the software for the robot and the paintings it would create. I automated a large, old-style drafting table so the carriage could

What a thrill back in 1981 to see the first robot's painting.

move up, down, left, and right along the table. The robotic wrist, brush, paints, and brush washer were mounted to the carriage. I taped down the canvas and propped it up at a slight angle. When finished, I framed that first painting created by the robot, and it hangs in my studio today.

I had a lot of fun building that robot and creating something new, but after evaluating my business plan, I realized that I couldn't cover my expenses and make enough profit for this to be a viable business. I wouldn't have known that had I not investigated my vision and done my homework. My vision was still alive; I just wasn't sure how to make it happen yet.

Doing Your Homework

The passions that form your vision will fall into one or more domains, and each domain requires special knowledge or abilities. How well versed are you in your applicable domains? There will also be practical considerations to making your vision real. For example, does your vision provide a viable path to income? What setup costs are involved, and how do you find customers or clients? This is all crucial information to explore before setting out on your fusioneer journey.

Alexander Fleming was a Scottish scientist studying infectious bacteria in 1928. He returned to his lab after time away to find mold growing in a petri dish that had been left out. That mold had killed off some of the bacteria. Fleming had stumbled upon a microbial defense system that became known as penicillin.

Serendipity, luck, and being in the right place at the right time have significantly influenced many great discoveries. While that is true and we don't know when inspiration will strike, we can properly set the stage by exploring and gaining knowledge within our chosen domains.

It's common for people to be more knowledgeable about one of the domains they hope to fuse. You can absolutely fuse domains that you aren't yet familiar with. The problem is that you might not be aware of the realities within that domain or its practical application in the real world. It's easy to form an impression or make assumptions that aren't entirely accurate. There might be some aspects you assume you'll love but don't enjoy them when you start. The opposite can be true as well, and you might love things within your chosen domains that you never anticipated. You never know until you poke around. That's why you want to take some time during this initial step to familiarize yourself with those domains that you aren't well versed in. That can involve studying in your spare time, finding online resources, talking with someone who works in that field, and even taking a class. Only by understanding your domains can you truly discover what is possible.

Would we have penicillin today if Fleming had not left out that petri dish? It's impossible to predict. However, Fleming was an expert in his domain who studied infectious bacteria in a lab, so he immediately recognized something out of the ordinary and had the instincts to investigate further. Would an auto mechanic who knew nothing about infectious bacteria have noticed the petri dish anomaly and discovered penicillin? Absolutely not, because the auto mechanic wouldn't be knowledgeable enough in that domain to know what to look for.

When formulating your vision, exploring your domains provides valuable insight, and determining the practicalities of making your vision a reality will be crucial. Here's how the three fusioneers we introduced in the previous chapter studied their respective domains.

Sarah

Before committing to becoming a ranching accountant, Sarah knew that she needed to do as much research as possible since her vision would require a major life change. The investigation began with the nature of her new work. Ranch accounting was different from the type of accounting she did back in Seattle, so she needed to explore the specifics of this new domain. While there were no traveling accountants who did exactly what she planned to do, there were plenty of accountants in Montana who specialized in this type of work. That meant she would have competition.

The next step was to figure out logistics, which involved where she would move and set up home base. Most ranches are a long drive from the nearest town, and that town is often so small it might not have professional services or even grocery stores. She needed to find a location that would put her in proximity to as many ranches as possible.

Having picked out a few locations, Sarah continued her investigation by testing the validity of her vision to determine if becoming a traveling accountant would give her a competitive advantage that could help her win clients. The simple way to do that was to call ranches to see if they were receptive to her ideas. These calls were also a way for her to gain as much information about her customers and competition as possible. What's so beneficial about this investigative process is that the more you learn, the more questions you think to ask. And the more people Sarah talked to, the more she recognized other types of accounting and tax advisory services that could help give her a competitive advantage.

With a much better understanding of the realities of what moving to Montana and starting this new business would involve, Sarah could then come up with a plan that put her in the best position to succeed. She learned that her vision was plausible, but that it could take a while for her to build the business. When getting started, she would need additional income, so she talked about her vision with one of the partners at her current firm with whom she had grown close. The partner was supportive, and together, they came up with an exit strategy that involved Sarah working remotely after making the move to Montana to build her new business. That took some of the pressure off. She then searched for local accounting firms in Montana who could serve as a stepping stone during her transition, while she learned the ins and outs of a new domain. At the very least, they could offer a fallback option if she needed more time to get her own business off the ground.

Tom

Tom was married with two kids and had a well-paying job when he formulated his vision to become a landscape designer. Much like Sarah, he couldn't afford to leave his job right away. He loved nature, architecture, and landscape, but he had never worked professionally in any of these domains before, so his upgrade would be significant. He started learning about landscape design in his free time and took an online class on weekends. That was a good introduction, but it couldn't replace hands-on experience. One obstacle for Tom was money. He didn't want to dip into the family savings. He also didn't have much free time.

With both his girls headed to summer camp and busy with their own activities, he developed a plan with his wife. He'd find a job on the weekends during the summer at a local nursery that was looking for seasonal help. That would allow him to learn more about plants while meeting potential customers and landscapers. There were still a lot of unknowns, so Tom sat down and came up with the following list of things he needed to learn:

- What services are offered by existing firms?
- How will his business be impacted by the seasons of the year?
- How long will each type of project take to complete?
- How will he be reimbursed for his up-front expenses?
- How do his competitors price their projects? What are their cost structures, and do they include any yearly maintenance and service contracts?
- What equipment and tools will he need to purchase in advance?

While working his part-time summer job, Tom learned the answers to all of these questions and many more. This investigative process helped him determine the size of his initial investment, while he gained a better understanding of market territories. He realized that his next step should involve seeking employment with an existing firm, so he could learn the business. It would have to be outside his target market because he would not want to compete with his employer for competition after branching out on his own. As a backup plan, he could establish a new market territory for his employer. That would give him access to their expertise and machinery. The more he immersed himself in the domain and researched his vision, the more ideas he developed and the more excited he became. It was clear that his vision was in direct alignment with his passions.

Noah

As a new college graduate, and not settled down to have a family or start a career, Noah had the fewest restrictions and responsibilities of these three fusioneers. That meant he had the most freedom, but that didn't exempt him from preparation. He calculated that he needed $5,000 saved before pursuing his vision of travel writing. That would require three more months of waiting tables.

In his spare time, Noah started researching all the possibilities that came with being a travel writer. In only a few weeks, he compiled a list of online publications and blogs that were open to submissions. He learned how much he could expect to make per article and what each site's policies were regarding contracts and expenses. He quickly got a feel for what locations and topics would appeal to readers and what types of articles were best suited for his vision. He started following and studying successful travel writers and read as many articles within his chosen domain as possible.

After learning that an existing writing portfolio (even nontravel articles) would be his biggest asset when earning future work, he tried to get as many freelance writing jobs as possible. Just as with Sarah and Tom, the more Noah learned, the more excited he became, and the more realistic his vision felt.

How Well Does Your Vision Fit into Your Life?

We all enter this process at different stages in life. Sarah is a young, single professional who has the freedom that Tom, who is married with two children about to enter college, does not. Noah has just graduated college, so he is younger and has more freedom than either of the other two.

Where are you at in your life? What is the status of your career and relationships? Doing your homework is your first step. Once you know more about how to execute your vision, the next step is understanding the impact this journey will have on your life and the lives of your loved ones. The following five items are a good checklist to help ensure you're taking everything into consideration before embarking on this journey.

Family

Start by looking at your family responsibilities and consider how this pursuit will impact those closest to you. If you're married and have children, you have certain commitments that those who are single don't. For those with a family, you want to discuss your vision and any possible sacrifices with them beforehand to gain their support, like Tom did with his nursery job. This way, you don't risk conflict down the road. No matter what the objective or dynamic, family and loved ones always work better when supporting each other as a team.

Career

What's great about fusioneering is that it can play different roles in your life, including possible career options. This can be liberating. It also raises the stakes and the level of risk, so pinpointing which route you plan to take will help determine the preparation required.

One option is using your fusioneer vision to replace a full-time job. This is a difficult path to take, because it involves changing jobs and perhaps even careers. Those who take this path have more at stake, which is why it requires more preparation and sacrifice. However, if you can make it work, this option allows you to fully focus on your fusion, without having to split your attention with another job.

As a second option, you might instead consider your vision as a second source of income. When taking this route, the stakes are lower, so this can alleviate some pressure. You aren't putting all your career eggs into a single basket, but you will also have to find time for your vision between work, family, and everything else in your life. However, with a serious focus on creating revenue from your vision, you can supplement your main source of income. That might eventually allow you to transition to the first option.

Finally, your vision may be something you pursue in your spare time for fun or to share with your loved ones. As with the second option, you'll have to make time for your vision amid your career and home life. But since you aren't relying on it for income, you have more freedom to explore and take chances.

Keep in mind that this is a fluid process. None of this is final. You might begin looking for a hobby or a way to reconnect with your passions in your spare time, only to later realize that you can turn your idea into a profitable business. That is very common, but when that time comes, you must do the same exploration to ensure you make your vision a plausible reality.

If you're entering this process completely open-minded and don't know exactly how you plan to use fusioneering, take money out of the equation, and wait to cross that bridge if you get there. For now, focus more on where you find passion, enjoyment, and purpose. As we get older, it becomes much easier to turn our backs on what we love in favor of making money and earning a living. That often leads to dissatisfaction and takes people on a roundabout journey that lands them back again, trying to reconnect with their passion. Don't force money into your exploratory process until it's necessary.

Financial Commitment

Even if you don't plan to use fusioneering to make money or earn a living, your vision might require a financial commitment. Money can heavily influence which undertaking you can realistically afford, so you want to budget accordingly. However, stepping-stone jobs within your domain are an excellent way to earn extra money that can help you pursue your vision while simultaneously learning the skills required to execute it. To determine if this is the right approach for you, you must consider the next item on the checklist.

Time Commitment

Time is the item that people most often miscalculate. We may plan to devote a certain amount of time to the pursuit of our vision only to discover that family and career responsibilities cut into that time. This investigatory phase of doing homework has the ancillary benefit of helping you understand how much time the pursuit of your vision will eventually require. For example, if, like Tom, you already work full time and have a family, by taking a stepping-stone job, you can figure out how to weave this pursuit into your already busy schedule. That's crucial when determining timelines and budgets. You don't want to plan an exit strategy from your current job only to later learn that you didn't give yourself enough time to investigate your vision.

Location

Can you execute your vision from where you currently live, or do you need to relocate? Sarah knew that she wanted to move to Montana to pursue her vision, so that factored into her timeline and budget. It required moving away from her family to a location where she only knew a few people and didn't have the same support system. For some people, this isn't a problem, but it might be difficult for others and could create additional stress and anxiety. No matter how comfortable you may be with a location change, it's always best to ease your way into a new environment and familiarize yourself with the area before fully committing.

With your vision fully formed and having poked around to familiarize yourself with the domains in which you'll be working, you can more accurately see how to incorporate fusioneering into your life. You are almost ready to move on to the next section and begin upgrading your skill set, but there is one more box you must tick before proceeding. It's arguably the most important step because, once achieved, it will be the fuel that propels you throughout the rest of the journey.

CHAPTER 4

You'll Know When You Know

Artist and architect Maya Lin was born to be a fusioneer. The beautiful opening line of her book *Boundaries* reads, "I feel I exist on the boundaries. Somewhere between science and art, art and architecture, public and private, east and west. I am always trying to find the balance between those opposing forces, finding the place where opposites meet."

Lin's parents fled China and settled in rural Ohio ten years before she was born, in 1959. When she was growing up, her parents never spoke about the past or where they came from. She didn't even realize she was Asian-American until college. She thought she was white, and part of that was because she was raised in a close-knit, insular family. It wasn't until later that she learned of her relatives' artistic and architectural achievements.

Both of her parents were professors who dabbled in the arts. Her mom was a poet, and her dad became a ceramist after moving to America. He made much of the furniture, plates, and bowls they used at home, so she grew up living and engaging with art in her everyday life. And there was no shortage of materials in the house to work with. She loved the three-dimensional process of sculpting and working with her hands the most. She spent much time alone and lost herself in art and the objects she created. She was someone who loved learning for the sake of learning.

If art was Lin's first passion, the environment was a close second. The way humans polluted the planet frightened her, but she found hope in the resilience of nature and the way it could be restored when people came together. She realized that when it comes to the earth, if people can't own it or see it, they tend to pollute it. That became the motivation behind her art and an essential piece of her journey. However, she never set out to become an artist. She considered going to school for zoology but didn't want to dissect dead animals, so she switched her major to architecture, because it combined math and art, two things she loved. That became her career path and area of study when she was accepted at Yale University.

A unique opportunity presented itself in 1981 when Lin was a senior at Yale. She entered an open contest to design the Vietnam Veterans Memorial in Washington, DC. She viewed it as an exercise and part of her senior project. She never thought she'd win, but that's precisely what happened.

Her memorial had a simplistic design, yet it was experiential and aesthetic. She viewed it as a work forged by cutting open the earth and repolishing the surface. While studying the nature of existing memorials, she realized that most war memorials were political statements made by the winning side about the victory. This one would be different. Since the veterans requested that it list the names of all 57,000 soldiers who went missing or died, Lin wanted to build the monument in honor of the individual. Politics had eclipsed what happened to the veterans, so this would be an apolitical statement about dealing with individual loss. For families to heal and the country to overcome the tragedy, they must first

Maya Lin

acknowledge the death that occurred, not pretend it didn't happen. Her approach would be honest. She wanted viewers to be able to read and touch every name.

Given her Asian ancestry and the fact she was a young woman, only twenty-one years old, her involvement was controversial. The submission process had been anonymous. The judges only knew her as applicant 1026. She never considered her background an issue until she was asked about it, which made her wonder if she would have won had her name been attached to her application. The process became a fight, and political hurdles had to be overcome, but in the end, the monument was built according to her vision. When the dust settled and the memorial was considered a success, she followed up her work in 1989 with the Civil Rights Memorial outside the Southern Poverty Law Center in Montgomery, Alabama, and then the Women's Table at Yale University in 1993.

Despite making a name for herself and developing a reputation as an architect, Lin felt conflicted and stuck between two identities. "You can be an architect or an artist, but you can't be both." That's what she was told in graduate school. Art was what she did every day. She never thought about it as a career. Only after graduating from the Yale School of Architecture did she realize that she thought like an artist. She pursued both art and architecture not because she chose to but because that's how she was wired. However, in our world of specialization, that wasn't an easy leap to make. Art and architecture are antithetical at times, and she feared that by pursuing multiple disciplines, she would never be seen as part of any realm or, worse, that the works themselves would be cluttered and confusing. It was advice from the architect Frank Gehry that finally helped her cast those doubts aside when he told her not to worry about the distinctions and just do the work. It was a struggle at first, but once she understood that she didn't have to choose and that she could exist between the boundaries, she finally felt whole.

Today, Maya Lin creates art, architecture, and memorials, all of which she uses to advocate for change—her purpose. She believes that each discipline needs to be sound and feels that you can't talk about one aspect of her work without talking about the others. It's an approach that epitomizes fusioneering.

No matter what the discipline, Lin is inspired by the beauty of nature and views the landscape like a cartographer. One natural element frequently appearing throughout her work is water—its boundary, surface, and what's below the surface. The San Francisco Bay, the waterways running under the state of Indiana, and even the mountain range below the ocean surface off the coast of Hawaii have all inspired her work. It was water along with the Native American burial grounds in her hometown and a symmetrical Stokes wave she saw when researching fluid dynamics that inspired *The Wave Field*. The piece is a 100-by-100-foot outdoor artwork located on a grass field at the University of Michigan.

While she knows her art will never recreate the beauty of the natural world, she strives to create work that points out aspects of nature people wouldn't typically notice. She wants the viewer to slow down, look at things in a new light, form their own opinion, and ultimately take action. Her architecture also combines elements of fusioneering by remaining connected to her environmental passions. She's ecologically responsible in the architectural projects she develops. When designing structures, she often blurs the dividing line between the inside and outside to keep the structure connected with the land.

Maya Lin is someone whose career doesn't follow the traditional linear trajectory. She forged her path by following her calling and didn't let anyone tell her what she could or couldn't do. It didn't come naturally at first. It had to germinate. Once she learned to fuse her passions, she found the freedom to pursue meaningful and enjoyable work while creating some of the most well-known pieces of art, memorials, buildings, and public spaces. Each piece of work is a separate vision that was created not from a bolt out of the blue but through a process of exploration.

Lin has said that she rarely arrives at an idea by consciously sitting at a desk and trying to figure out what she wants to do next. However, once she begins thinking about a project, she remains focused until she comes up with an idea. That can take years, and when that happens, she knows immediately. In other words, when she knows, she knows. That can all be traced back to internal motivation.

Internal versus External Motivation

There is an unspoken bond between Harvard Business School graduates, even among those who have never met. Bill was one of those people. He was a money manager from Boston with an extensive art collection whom I met while working as a part-time ski instructor in Vail, Colorado. He was a little older than I was, but whenever I saw him, he always asked me the same question: "Paul, how much money do I need to retire?"

Each time, I'd tell him the same thing: "Bill, you already have enough money to retire. You just have to figure out what you want to do next."

Over multiple years, we probably had that same exchange three different times, but I never said what he wanted to hear, so he kept asking. Given what I knew about Bill, money was the yardstick by which he measured almost everything. We never talked about what he enjoyed. Even when he discussed art, it was never about the art itself but framed within the context of money. To him, making money was the goal. He probably liked what he was doing and was good at it. He appeared to live comfortably, but his repeated question suggested he wanted something else. The problem was that he didn't have a vision or a purpose, so he had no idea what he should pursue next.

Bill's attitude was, "I'll be able to finally do *X* when I complete *Y*." This is an attitude that many have when it comes to their work and what they believe will bring them fulfillment. Instead, it leaves them feeling unfulfilled. The reason is twofold. First, they haven't discovered their purpose, their dharma or reason for being. Second, they haven't learned the distinction between being externally and internally motivated.

In his essay "The Bus Ticket Theory of Genius," computer scientist and essayist Paul Graham deconstructs what he believes to be a common trait among those who have done great work. Believe it or not, some people collect bus tickets. It's a hobby pursued not for fame or fortune but out of curiosity and what Graham describes as an "obsessive interest." Whether collecting comic books, stamps, art, or bus tickets, it requires that obsessive interest to dive into the minutiae of certain topics that most people wouldn't bother to notice. These collectors don't care what anyone else thinks about what they do. The journey itself provides their internal motivation, and that's what it means to be autotelic. That word derives from Greek—*auto* ("self") and *telos* ("goal"). It means being internally driven by a sense of purpose, as opposed to being externally driven by an outcome or reward. The joy and fulfillment come from the journey, not getting to the end of the rainbow.

In addition to autotelic motivation, if you look closely at many who changed the world, you will often see that insatiable curiosity inspired them to spend hours exploring their domain and honing their skills. An excellent example is one of the first Renaissance men and the person who became my icon and role model, Leonardo da Vinci.

Leonardo had a rare talent, and I marvel at what he accomplished. I also marvel at the depths of his curiosity and internal drive, because I believe that is what truly enabled him to be great. In his biography of da Vinci, Walter Isaacson says that Leonardo "willed his way to genius" and points out how his curiosity, acute ability to observe, childlike wonder, careful attention to detail, and openness to mystery were most responsible for his achievements. That is all the result of being autotelic, or internally motivated.

There is nothing wrong with external motivation. However, it can also cover up the source of our dissatisfaction and fool us into thinking we're doing what we really want to be doing. When I finish *X*, I can finally focus on *Y* often means that when I get done with what I *have to do*, I can finally focus on what I *want to do*. The typical nine-to-five grind often reinforces this thinking. When living like this for so long, it can take a tremendous amount of energy to suddenly look at things from a different point of view. That doesn't mean it can't happen. It just requires a mindset shift, and there is a secret. It's something we've already discussed—purpose.

The reason purpose has been mentioned so often throughout this section is that, when your vision incorporates your purpose, it's much easier to become autotelic. When you are autotelic, it's harder to turn your back on what you love and fall victim to the societal pressures to make money or achieve status. When you are autotelic, you look forward to putting in the extra work because you aren't focused on the end result; you are focused on the journey. In that mindset, you are capable of achieving great things. It's what Maya Lin felt when she finally realized that she no longer had to choose between art, architecture, and sculpture; she could exist between the boundaries. It would be what I felt when I set out on my journey. However, before I committed, I first needed to experience my second epiphany.

My Second Epiphany

After working in marketing at HP, I found success as a venture capitalist, investing in early-stage high-tech companies. All the while, I never forgot that first epiphany on the footbridge in 1977. I may have shelved the original idea, but I still wanted to pursue my vision of fusing art and science. On October 13, 1993, I wrote the following:

> Throughout history, man's art has been a temporal reflection of his own culture and society. His art often outlived him, some of which transcended through time and remains an expression and testament of his era.
>
> What I would like to do is combine the machine age, the computer age, artificial intelligence, and art to create actual full-sized paintings. The machine age component is expressed through motors and robotics, incorporating sensory feedback and electronic controls to produce actual paintings with canvas, brush, and paint. The computer age component uses a Silicon Graphics workstation running Franz Inc.'s Lisp and CLOS. This is coupled to an Adept Technology robot

> controller and vision system, running their proprietary real-time multitasking, multiple-axis, machine-control operating system. The artificial intelligence component incorporates contemporary theories of adaptively intelligent learning systems, genetic algorithms, and genetic programming to breed selectively more robust and capable artistically orientated lifeforms. The art component, residing inside the population of intelligent lifeforms and expressed on canvas, uses principles of fine art, including composition, color, value, brushwork, and texture.
>
> Hopefully, after several years of effort, the paintings will creatively stand on their own merit and will be commanding to behold and magnificent to view.

Everything changed in January 1994, when I experienced my second epiphany, and it all started with an impromptu invite from an old friend.

Lars was a member of the Royal Danish Air Force. I met him in the second grade, when I lived in Denmark, and we became lifelong friends. We sailed together in the ocean around Copenhagen, and he'd often visit me in Colorado to go skiing. Lars lived an amazing life. He joined the Royal Danish Air Force out of high school and worked his way up through the ranks to become the chief of a helicopter crew that conducted rescue missions at sea. By the end of his career, he had completed over one thousand life-saving missions. He was friends with the crown prince and was awarded the Danish equivalent of the Congressional Medal of Honor for heroism. He was an impressive guy who has since passed away from brain cancer.

In January 1994, Lars invited me to ski with him in Europe. Our initial plan was to drive from his home in Copenhagen down to Saalbach, Austria. Before we set out, he suggested we take the ferry the next day to Malmo, Sweden, to visit the Leonardo da Vinci traveling museum exhibit.

While Lars had lived with the crew in a barracks near the helicopter landing pad, he was on call twenty-four hours a day for many days in a row. During his downtime, he ran a small auto repair business out of a single-car garage that he rented. He was always good at working with his hands. He liked to tinker with simple household items and to build things. Like me, he enjoyed inventing and designing stuff, so it was natural that he was interested in da Vinci.

I had a general knowledge of da Vinci. I knew about the *Mona Lisa* and *The Last Supper*, but I wasn't prepared to be so impacted by this exhibit. It was roughly the size of a basketball court. I was mesmerized by the notebook on display in a glass case and the beautiful wooden replicas of his mechanical inventions. There was a rich variety of functional designs. What inspired me most was the depth and breadth of his intense creative energy. Thinking of the intellectual prowess and imagination it took to create his paintings and to design these machines overwhelmed and inspired me. I had seen pictures and read books, but to view these creations right there in front of me was a once-in-a-lifetime experience. Other people walked in and walked out, but I was mesmerized. That got me thinking: *What if da Vinci were alive today and wanted to combine his love of technology with art? What would that look like?*

That was all the fuel I needed. Something inside me dramatically changed, and that experience altered the trajectory of my life. I left the museum knowing I had to follow through on my dream that began when I crossed that footbridge over the Charles River in 1977. I wouldn't have had the same reaction if the exhibit had been about only his art. I might have written about it in my notebook and fumbled around, but I probably never would have been fully committed. Returning home, that exhibit created the excitement and inspiration I needed to move forward.

Shortly thereafter, I moved from Boulder to Loveland, Colorado, to be part of the town's vibrant art community. Loveland is considered the sculpting capital of North America. Adjacent to a large bronze foundry, one of four in the area, was an excellent, nationally known art school where I attended classes and weeklong workshops. Across the parking lot were ten studios in a row, all designed for north light. At that time, I was able to lease one of the four new studios under construction and, for a one-time charge, had the builder install extra utility power in my unit. I knew I would need that for what I had in mind. When construction was completed in April 1994, that's when my fusioneering journey really started. I was so excited to finally be following my dharmic dream.

Your vision will become your source of energy as you pursue your reason for being. This journey will become your true source of fulfillment. With your newly formed vision, you can move to the next step: upgrading.

IRELAND
EST. 1840

Typical scene of Glenn teaching in a museum

PART 2

UPGRADE

With your vision fully formed, it's time to become proficient in the skills required to execute that vision. Upgrading is about preparation. This is the learning phase of the process, which will be ongoing throughout your journey.

Consider the legs of your stool. Your vision is the seat, and the legs are the domains and interests you hope to fuse. Each leg will require certain skills, some of which you may need to upgrade. Your next step is to improve your skills for each leg to the level you'll need in order to move forward with your vision.

Upgrading is a highly personalized process. In the beginning, not all of your skill levels will be equal. That's to be expected. Each skill set is unique. Some may upgrade quickly, while others may take longer. It depends entirely on your current skill level and the level of proficiency you need to reach that particular skill. You need to develop a skill only to the level required to execute your vision. And the way you develop that skill set will be unique to you. In this section, I'll explain different learning styles and various upgrading techniques that will help you organize this phase of your journey.

At this stage, it's important to realize you don't know what you don't know. No matter how much investigation and research you did in part 1, it is impossible to plan for everything. Once you start down this path and learn more about particular domains, you might realize that upgrading certain skills is more involved or might take longer than anticipated. After some initial work, you might also discover you need to add an additional leg or two to your stool, and those legs might require you to upgrade a new set of skills. Problems will arise, and plans will go awry. Resources you've come to rely on might no longer be available, finances might become tight, or your initial assumptions might prove to be erroneous. This is all to be expected. Enter this stage with an open mind and be willing to adapt when necessary.

Your vision will be your guide throughout this journey. If forced to alter your path, refer back to the work you did in part 1. Remain true to your core intelligences and the actions from your Seven Stories, because that's what lights you up inside. Indulge your interests, and lean into your strengths. It's not about getting through this stage quickly. It's about preparing yourself as well as possible for the journey ahead.

Remember that upgrading should be enjoyable because you are doing what you love and already living your dream. Make sure you take time to pause once in a while and just enjoy the moment!

CHAPTER 5

Planning Your Upgrade

Before you begin, you must first determine the skills that require upgrading. After closely examining the legs of my stool, I came up with a list of seven skills that I needed to develop.

- Learn more about art and how to paint.
- Learn about the hardware needed to build the robot.
- Learn machine shop skills to make the parts for the robot.
- Learn about the electronics needed to power the robot.
- Learn about the industrial computer and operating system to configure and run the robot.
- Learn about the V+ robot coding required to run the robot.
- Learn high levels of coding, including AI, to create the art for the robot to paint.

One of the many legs of Paul's stool—his love of art

All these skills were essential, and some I was much more familiar with than others. It's important to understand that this list is just a starting point. The fusioneering process is inherently flexible, so as you progress along your journey, you might discover you need to develop additional skills.

While determining the skills you need to upgrade may happen quickly, developing them so you can reach the required level of proficiency may take much longer. You want to make that process as natural and enjoyable as possible. The best way to do that is to ensure that you're learning in a way that works for you.

How Do You Learn?

There are different ways to learn, and knowing your preferred style will help you plan your upgrade. Even if you think you have it all figured out, answer the following questions. You might be surprised by the ways in which you learn.

If you need directions to a nearby location, what would be the ideal way for you to get that information?

- Ask a friend to tell you.
- Refer to a map or GPS.
- Write down directions.

If given instructions for making a spreadsheet, what is your ideal way to get that information?

- Watch the person create the graph first.
- Listen to what they are saying.
- Look at the diagram.
- Read the instructions.

When learning a new skill, how do you prefer to receive that information?

- Watch a video.
- Receive written instructions.
- Listen to an instructor during a presentation.
- Participate in a workshop.

If you suffer from a health problem, how would you like the doctor to explain your condition?

- Sit you down and walk you through the issue.
- Give you something to read.
- Refer to a visual model.
- Refer to a video.

When deciding where to invest your money, what would be the best way to arrive at your decision?

- Talk with experts.
- Read articles.
- Study charts and graphs.
- Rely on trial and error.

Working as a part-time ski instructor in Vail, Colorado, was when I first understood people had different ways of learning.

After skiing the mountain for more than twenty years, I wanted a new adventure and an opportunity to meet people, so I set out to become a part-time ski instructor in 1995. In addition to the training we received in Vail Ski School, it was recommended that all new instructors join PSIA (Professional Ski Instructors of America) and go through their extensive training and testing to become certified. During this training process, I was taught four ways people could learn:

- Watching
- Thinking
- Doing
- Feeling

When teaching on the slopes, I quickly realized that when I adjusted my approach to fit my student's learning style, it significantly accelerated their progress, while reducing their frustration. It also increased their level of enjoyment throughout the process.

Picture a family of four who arrive at ski school one morning to take a family lesson. After a warm-up run or two, I tell them, "I'll ski down first to that blue sign. One at a time, you can follow me." Once we are together again, I ask each about their run and listen to the verbs they use to describe their experience.

The husband says that he thought about the ski tip I casually offered him while we were chatting on the chair ride up. His wife says she watched me as I skied down the mountain. The young daughter talks about feeling the weight on her outside leg, and the teenage son doesn't have much to say because he just skied down the mountain.

It may not sound like much information, but I now had some clues for how to help them improve. I could immediately tell that the husband was a thinker, who would respond well to explanations. The wife was a watcher, who would do well by observing and following me. The daughter was a feeler, who would best be served by me describing the proper sensations she should feel. The son was a doer. I would just leave him alone to do his thing.

Those four verbs—thinking, watching, feeling, and doing—were how I adjusted my coaching to fit any student. And realizing that someone might have more than one learning style, I made sure to use multiple approaches for each person as the day progressed.

You may be wondering what learning style or styles you might have. I wondered that too. I instinctively thought I was a thinker first and then a feeler. During that first learning-style lecture, we were given a twenty-question, multiple-choice quiz. I was amazed when I learned I scored a perfect twenty for visual. In retrospect, it makes sense since I love art, was good at math, and always liked building things, but I sure had no idea before that moment.

There are other models. For example, Neil Fleming developed the VARK model in 1987, which is laid out next. A great way to determine which of the following categories you fit into is to think back to how you learned best when in school.

Visual

If you paid more attention to the teacher's whiteboard than the textbook, you might be a visual learner. That means you best retain information by seeing it. This could entail watching someone rather than hearing information, reading, or doing the actual task. If you're this type of learner, charts, illustrations, videos, images, and demonstrations are useful.

Auditory

If you were a person who found lectures more valuable than textbooks when in school, you're probably an auditory learner. These learners tend to easily and accurately repeat back information that someone told them. They best retain information when they hear it, so lectures, podcasts, and tutoring fit this learning style. Auditory learners often work best in quiet environments.

Reading and Writing

If you paid more attention to textbooks than lectures, your learning style might center on reading and writing. In addition to devouring written material, these learners take excessive notes. They are often good storytellers. This type of learner works best when away from distractions.

Kinesthetic

Those who prefer a hands-on approach are typically kinesthetic learners, or people who learn by doing. They tend to gravitate toward physical activities and trades, such as carpentry, electricity, and even cooking. Shop class, home economics, or gym are favorites of kinesthetic learners. This type of learning requires movement, physical practice, and sometimes just using your hands.

Whether you identify with the PSIA approach or VARK, by understanding your learning styles, you'll use your time more efficiently, while cutting down on potential frustration. It's equally important to understand which type of learner you are not. If you have trouble retaining information when you read, struggle to concentrate, or don't find reading enjoyable, seek other ways to obtain knowledge. If you're a visual learner, you'd be better served watching videos and listening to lectures in your area of study or creating flash cards than reading through a stack of books on the same subject.

Determining your learning styles makes it easier to schedule your upgrade and integrate it into your daily routine. For example, if you are an auditory learner who easily retains information when listening, you can benefit from podcasts and audiobooks. This can be a great way to multitask. So if you have a commute or frequently do lengthy cardio sessions at the gym, you can listen to material relevant to your upgrade. If you have children, a full-time job, or other outside responsibilities, it can be difficult to find the time required to upgrade your skill sets, so a better understanding of how to use your learning styles to your advantage can make this process more efficient and effective. Everyone's situation and upgrade are different, so make sure you're doing what's best for you and are utilizing all the tools at your disposal.

What you don't want to do is pigeonhole yourself as one type of learner. There is a good chance you fit it into multiple categories, or your learning style may differ with the task. This can have a lot to do with the type of skill you need to upgrade, as not all learning styles are conducive to every skill set. You might find that one style works best to upgrade your skills in one discipline and that another style is best for another discipline.

Your Path Forward

Given my professional experience, I was used to creating workflow charts. So when I set out to build the robot and fuse art, science, and robotics, I made a chart of all the things I had to do and in sequence. The result left me feeling so overwhelmed. I couldn't picture myself living that way for the next five, ten, or however many years it would take. I said, "This isn't going to work for me." I was miserable and felt depressed for days. I wanted to pursue my dream, but I knew I couldn't proceed this way. That's when I realized that I didn't have to do it that way.

I discarded the charts, didn't worry about reaching milestones, and simply decided that, each day, I would go where my energy took me. That became my path forward, and that path has happily guided me for more than twenty-five years. When people visit the studio, I like to talk about what I'm working on at that moment, because that's where my energy is, and not necessarily discuss any earlier painting or technology.

I've been following my energy since I was a kid. At HP Labs, my boss would give me an assignment and I'd run with it. Often, what materialized was nothing that would've ever shown up on a chart at the beginning. There was no way I could have anticipated all the twists, turns, and evolutions the process would take. You just don't know the result until you get there. The same is true today regarding my fusioneering journey and the artwork I create.

I've learned that as long as I'm following my passion, and continually striving forward, the outcome is achievable, and may well pass my initial expectations. It may sound daunting, but what keeps me going is that energy and enthusiasm. Once I tapped into that, I never experienced another bad day at work again, because I absolutely love what I do.

There is freedom in fusioneering, but that doesn't mean the process is completely without structure or direction. There will be more to learn and skills to improve. Going forward, here are two questions to consider:

- What's my current skill level?
- Where does that level need to be to execute my vision?

With a better understanding of your learning styles and a clear grasp of what level of proficiency you need to achieve within each of the skill sets, you can begin to develop a plan. In the next chapter, we'll consider various methods and techniques that you can apply when on your journey.

CHAPTER 6

Developing Your Skills

Each of the legs of your stool represents a domain of knowledge you need that supports your vision. Therefore, you must achieve a level of proficiency for each of these to successfully move forward. We outline a few methods here.

Self-Development

Depending upon the skill set needed, self-development might be an easy place to start. Then later, if additional help is needed, there are viable alternatives.

Noah continued working at a restaurant as a waiter while upgrading his skills to become a travel writer. When he began his upgrade, he set out to further develop his writing skills and come up with a plan regarding travel logistics (where he would go, what he would write about, and how much it would cost). When not waiting tables, he devoted his energy to those two areas. He was young, single, fresh out of college, and energetic, so nothing held him back, and he could freely travel when the time was right.

Further Develop Writing Skill

Noah was already earning a small income in one of these disciplines by working as a freelance writer. He had two clients and wrote a couple of short articles and blog posts a week for each. The jobs didn't pay much, and it wasn't travel writing, but he was honing his skill. He was also learning how to write in different styles and incorporate feedback while meeting deadlines, all crucial skills if he was to become a professional writer. It was difficult for him at first, and it took him a long time to complete even one article, but he remained persistent.

One crucial aspect of Noah's upgrade was studying the work of other writers who wrote similar content. He quickly learned the elements of compelling writing, which he applied to his own work. He also read plenty of articles that weren't up to par, and when comparing them with the more popular articles, he better understood what not to do. The more he read, the more he recognized his positive and negative tendencies as a writer and was able to eliminate his bad habits.

In only a few months, Noah could already tell that his writing had improved, and he was able to complete assignments faster. He was also becoming well versed in the business of freelance writing. The more Noah worked, the bigger his portfolio became. He was then able to use those samples to find a third client who paid him a little more money per article. This client required a different style and type of writing, but Noah was now able to more easily adapt because he had become a versatile writer. That boosted his confidence, and he realized that he could adapt his style while learning how to satisfy potential client needs. More important, he was enjoying himself.

Two legs of Paul's stool—math and art

Travel Logistics

When he was young, Noah loved learning about other cultures and civilizations. That's what gave him the itch to travel the world. He already knew Brazil was at the top of his list. Having been fascinated with the Amazonian culture since childhood, he now wanted to backpack through the country, so he could meet the locals and learn about their customs.

Noah easily generated a list of travel destinations and potential writing ideas. That was the fun part. However, seeing what was practical and would fit within his budget was not nearly as fun. He had to face some harsh realities regarding his vision when it came to finances and budgeting.

Until he crunched the numbers, he never realized how quickly expenses added up. During his initial research, he drastically underestimated how much lodging, meals, and travel between locations would actually cost. Without additional income, his savings could quickly evaporate, which would shorten the amount of time he could spend in Brazil, thus narrowing his window to get consistent work as a travel writer. He quickly got to work, looking for ways to economize and cut down on expenses.

What made Noah's situation more difficult was that he wouldn't be able to earn income as a travel writer until he had actually traveled and written articles. Even then, he needed to find clients who would publish or post his work. He had made inquiries and had a few leads to go on when he had the material ready to submit, but having learned a lot about the freelance writing business in the past few months, he understood how difficult it would be to earn a livable income solely as a travel writer. That being said, he believed in himself and knew he was capable of doing the job. It would just take some time. This weighed heavily on his mind and made him nervous. Being creative, he came up with two potential solutions.

The first was simple: He would try to find more freelance writing clients. The beautiful thing about freelance writing was that he could do it from anywhere in the world. All he needed was a laptop and an internet connection. It didn't matter if he wasn't yet writing content related to his travel vision. With enough clients paying him to write articles, he could earn a steady income that could support him while in Brazil indefinitely. This eliminated the ticking clock and would allow him to transition naturally into full-time travel writing whenever the opportunity presented itself. More writing jobs also meant that he could improve his skill while creating additional samples to help him obtain more work. It was an excellent way for him to gain experience and build momentum as a professional writer.

The second idea was more of a backup plan. Noah had been a waiter and worked in restaurants throughout his time at college, so he had extensive experience. There were restaurants all over Brazil, and many in the bigger cities catered to Americans. It wasn't a sure thing, but he saw the opportunity to go back to waiting tables if he ever found himself in a financial bind. Most important, this gave him some much-needed peace of mind.

It took Noah about four months to complete this phase of his upgrade. He had done his homework, crunched the numbers, and created a plan that put him in the best possible position to succeed. He even doubled his freelance writing income by taking on more clients that he would continue working for in South America. He gave himself two more months to earn extra money and continue developing his freelance writing skills. He moved out of his apartment and back in with his family to save a little more, and he set a date when he would officially leave for South America.

After graduating college, Noah was living on a budget, so he didn't have money to spend on his upgrade. However, he didn't view this as an obstacle. Using his laptop, he could access all the information required for his upgrade, and he could do it all without spending a single dollar or receiving any outside help. Depending on your vision, it's likely that you too have many free resources at your disposal. Don't underestimate what you can accomplish on your own.

Stepping-Stone Jobs

A stepping-stone job offers several advantages as you acquire knowledge for your respective domains. You can start slowly and assimilate knowledge naturally. As you ease in, you'll learn things you might not have thought about or appreciated the extent and depth of knowledge needed. This hands-on experience can accelerate your learning while at the same time providing a supplemental income. Associating with people who enjoy this domain certainly has its inherent benefits.

Tom continued to work full-time as a data scientist for a software company while he completed his upgrade. He needed to focus on three areas: landscaping, business ownership, and client outreach.

Even though Tom was trying to transition into a new domain and career where he had no professional experience, he knew he'd be doing what he loved. According to the intelligence exercise, his vision was in line with the actions that came naturally to him. Growing up fishing in Colorado fostered his love of nature, and the architecture class he took in college exposed his love of visual design. He was also good at math. Fuse them all together, and landscape architecture is closely linked to his passion and his nature, even though he'd never worked a job in this field. Tom was married with children, so he had to proceed cautiously. He worked with his spouse to devise a careful plan going forward.

Learning about Landscaping

Once Tom's kids were away at camp for the summer, he went to work at the local nursery on weekends as he had arranged a few weeks earlier. He wasn't doing it for the money; he wanted to learn, and he was someone who learned by doing.

Going in, Tom knew he had a lot to learn. However, he did not anticipate learning as much and as quickly as he did. Every day he was surrounded by the plants, materials, and tools of the trade. He was a sociable guy, and talking with the owners and customers came naturally to him. He became friendly with some of the regular customers and got to know the local contractors and landscapers as well. As part of his job, he made deliveries to various job sites. Seeing the stages of landscape design, noting how the bushes and trees were installed, and watching the workers use the equipment proved to be an unexpected and invaluable learning experience.

When Tom and his wife purchased their home, he put time and effort into caring for their lawn. It became a passion. Once he started learning more about landscape architecture, he realized there was much more to the craft than caring for a lawn and installing some shrubs. It went beyond plants, soils, fertilizers, and sprinkler systems. There was an important landscaping plan, which outlined the overall design and itemized planting locations. It was about the little things too, like the placement of certain plants according to color, and when they bloom. Bushes, trees, and rocks of different shapes and sizes needed to be strategically placed to help create a rich tapestry of texture and movement for the eye.

The more he was around these job sites, the more he learned. He started carrying around a small pocket notebook to write down his ideas and always returned home with a list of topics to research. At night, he watched YouTube videos and found a number of creators whose content he devoured in his spare time.

Learning How to Become a Business Owner

Having never started or owned a business, Tom felt overwhelmed when trying to upgrade this skill set. What he mistakenly assumed would be the easiest part of his upgrade proved to be the most difficult. By the end of the summer, Tom had learned a lot working at the nursery, but he wasn't any closer to understanding what it took to run a successful landscaping business. He needed a new stepping-stone job and saw the perfect opportunity to continue his upgrade.

While making deliveries, Tom befriended Hector, the owner of a successful landscaping business. Hector was in his sixties and had spent the previous thirty years building his business from the ground up. He had a few private clients whose lawns he designed, but most of his clients were companies who hired him to design and install landscaping for their properties. By the end of the summer, Tom and Hector would often meet after work on a Friday for a beer as they got to know each other very well. Tom was up front about his long-term goals and knew that Hector wanted to retire in a few years, so he made a proposition: What if Hector took him under his wing and trained him in the business, so Tom could buy him out in a few years?

Hector liked Tom. He looked forward to retirement, but he

also wanted to make sure his business was in good hands when he stepped away. He saw that Tom was passionate and eager to learn, so he agreed. When Tom's part-time nursery job came to an end in August, he gave notice at his old firm and soon went to work for Hector full time.

Client Outreach

Tom realized it would be difficult for him to secure enough clients to run a successful business. He didn't have the experience or the reputation, and in order to retain new clients, he'd probably have to take them from other landscapers. He knew he wasn't ready yet, so the partnership with Hector was the perfect opportunity. He could learn the business, and when Hector retired, he would be taking over a successful operation with a good reputation that already had employees, vendors, and clients.

Over the next five years, Tom significantly upgraded his skills. He worked with vendors to place orders and even began working with potential clients. He got to know them and would consider their vision and wish list before bidding on the project. He learned to develop detailed plans for the customer to review, so he could bring their vision to life. He enjoyed articulating the aesthetic qualities he used in his designs. This suited his personality and allowed him to demonstrate his visual design abilities.

Tom's story is a great example of how you can hone your vision during your upgrade. I can't emphasize enough that when you're on this journey, you don't know what you don't know, so as you learn more about the domains you hope to fuse, you will inevitably encounter issues and obstacles. Some people will work through those obstacles in time, while others may have to adapt their vision. The more familiar you become with your domains, the easier it will be to recognize those moments when they occur.

As Hector neared retirement, Tom felt confident in his ability to take over and grow the business. More than five years had passed since he solidified his vision. His upgrade took much longer than he initially planned, but because he adjusted his vision, he was now much better prepared to become a business owner. Much of that success can be attributed to his stepping-stone jobs that allowed him to slowly transition out of his previous career and into his new one naturally, without having to risk his family's financial future. Stepping-stone jobs are an excellent way to upgrade your skills while earning extra money and gradually phasing into your next stage.

Mentors

You don't need to go on this journey alone. While your fusioneering vision may be unique, the domains you're operating in are most likely well established and ripe with experts. If you can learn from one or more of those experts and receive the benefit of them taking you under their wing, it can significantly improve the speed and efficiency of your upgrade. Mentorship is a proven way to develop one's skills, and it's a method even the masters benefited from before they became masters.

Born out of wedlock in a small town just outside of Florence, Italy, in 1452, Leonardo da Vinci was raised primarily by his grandparents. That meant he wasn't sent to one of the Latin schools to receive a traditional education, so Leonardo was primarily self-taught from an early age. In his notebook he wrote, "They will say that because I have no book learning, I cannot properly express what I desire to describe, but they do not know that my subjects require experience rather than the words of others." The lack of a formal education wasn't a problem for Leonardo. It suited his curious nature, and he wasn't afraid to question conventional wisdom, but it's important to understand that he didn't learn everything on his own. He benefited from mentorship as a young man, which helped shape the trajectory of his life and pursuits.

From an early age, Leonardo had a passion for drawing and sculpting. When it came time for him to learn a trade at the age of twelve, he moved to Florence with Ser Piero, his father. Piero, a local notary, chose not to legitimize his son because, given the custom of the time, it would inevitably mean that he, too, would become a notary. It was obvious that Leonardo was not meant to be a notary, and he found himself in the perfect location to cultivate his rare artistic talents.

Florence was a cultural and artistic melting pot. It was a center of commerce and entertainment. Professionals dabbled in multiple disciplines, so using the various tools at their disposal, artists were often also architects. Given the nature of his profession, Piero rubbed shoulders with some of Florence's most prominent artists and teachers. In 1467, he found the perfect mentor for Leonardo in Andrea del Verrocchio, who operated and oversaw a workshop that employed multiple artisans who produced the art sold by the workshop. When Verrocchio viewed the drawings made by young Leonardo, he agreed to take the boy on as an apprentice.

These workshops were a common way for young artists to hone their craft. The Italian painter Cennino Cennini wrote extensively about the apprenticeship process during the 1430s. He believed that the process should take thirteen years, during which the young artist places himself in servitude to the master. It begins with completing humble tasks and making very little money while the artist works his way up from apprentice to journeyman and then finally to master craftsman. That's how Verrocchio got his start. When growing up, he first apprenticed under a goldsmith and evolved into a sculptor, even replacing the esteemed Donatello as the sculptor to the powerful Medici family.

In 1467, Verrocchio's workshop operated in a similar manner and was considered a university of the arts. Located on the street among the people, it was a popular meeting place for artistic youths. The artists and apprentices all lived under the same roof and ate

Andrea del Verrocchio, Leonardo da Vinci's mentor in Florence

most of their meals together. The workshop ran almost like a factory, with artists applying their specialty to various projects. Many of the works of art produced were collaborations. This included paintings but also sculptures, most notably an elegant four-foot bronze sculpture of David. Leonardo's tutelage under Verrocchio wasn't only in art. He learned a wide array of disciplines during his time at the workshop.

Soon after Leonardo's arrival at the workshop, Verrocchio was commissioned to install the tombstone in the Church of San Lorenzo for Cosimo de' Medici, known as "The Father of the State." That further developed Verrocchio's reputation, and he received additional commissions. He then expanded his work to include painting and decorating. Most notably, he was commissioned to serve as engineer and contractor (in addition to artist) when creating and installing a two-ton copper ball to place on top of Brunelleschi's cathedral dome in Florence. The dome had been under construction since before 1300 and is an astonishing piece of fusioneering that we will discuss later. It's believed by many that this project is what began Leonardo's fascination with machinery.

While serving as an apprentice, Leonardo's constant experimentation introduced him to other elements that found their way into his work. At the time, pageants and plays were the most popular form of entertainment. As an additional form of income, the workshop frequently developed decorations and art for these events. One of the most significant was in honor of the Duke of Milan in 1471. During this time, Leonardo developed a brand-new obsession for theater. He experimented with costumes, scenery, stage machinery, and special effects, thus blending his love of art with engineering.

Leonardo's apprenticeship ended in 1472, when he turned twenty, but he continued to work in Verrocchio's studio as a master painter. Verrocchio was the first person outside Leonardo's immediate family to significantly influence the young artist. Seventeen years older than Leonardo, Verrocchio was a true mentor who helped Leonardo expand his skill set. That is most likely why he remained at the studio for such a long period. However, Leonardo's early works show evidence of skill that goes beyond that of his master. In 1477, Leonardo felt it was time to venture out on his own.

If you have the access and the means, learning from professionals and experts in a given discipline can be a great opportunity for you. Even a local class, teacher, professional, or online course might provide valuable insight and guidance.

Networking

Networking adds an additional and dynamic alternative method for upgrading your skills. Unforeseen opportunities might emerge that make merry with the self-development, stepping-stone, and mentoring techniques just mentioned.

While continuing to work at her Seattle accounting firm full-time, Sarah simultaneously began her upgrade. She needed to focus on three areas: learning more about ranch accounting, figuring out the area where she'd be working and living, and preparing to start her business.

Although she had more than a decade of experience as an accountant, she needed to learn about the specific requirements of ranch accounting. She could do this from home, but she needed to travel to Montana ranch country to get the answers to the rest of her many questions. Where was the best place to live that would put her in proximity to as many ranches as possible? How could she develop her brand-new business? What specific accounting services would potential clients want? How could she meet with them, gain their trust, and then win them over as clients? How would she compete with existing accounting firms? Most significantly, would her original travel accountant idea that was conceived at the wedding give her a competitive advantage? Sarah already had some ideas from when she did her earlier homework; now, she had to confirm those and develop her skills further.

Learning about Ranch Accounting

Sarah was already a good accountant. She had a solid foundation, so it didn't take long to learn the specific requirements and peculiarities of ranch accounting. There were plenty of resources at her disposal, and she even spoke with a few colleagues and professionals who had specific expertise in this area. One in particular was very skilled in this area and willing to assist her. The additional, specific accounting skills needed were straightforward, and it took her only four weeks to grasp them.

Ranch and Home Logistics

Taking a week of vacation days, Sarah packed up her Jeep and drove nine hours from Seattle to Helena, Montana. She planned to spend a few days there before continuing to Bozeman and then Billings. She didn't need to visit Montana to know that there was a lot of open country and that the ranches were spread out. Still, her first official scouting visit was an eye-opening experience about just how big Big Sky Country really was.

Before moving to Montana, Sarah needed to figure out the optimal location for her new business venture. To be a traveling accountant, she needed easy access to as many ranches as possible. However, many of these ranches were not easy to get to, often located at the end of long dirt roads that went on for miles. One rancher lived so far away from town that he told Sarah how he and his wife had to carefully plan the trip to the hospital when their first son was born.

While out there in the country, Sarah learned of another major obstacle she hadn't thought of during her initial research: snow. Seattle got lots of rain but not snow. She learned that, during the winter, it was common for some of these ranches to be snowed in for days and even weeks at a time. Being able to reach these ranches and access her clients during winter could be difficult if she wasn't prepared.

Sarah had set up meetings with some accountants in the towns and with ranchers in the open country. She was shocked that almost everyone she reached out to agreed to either meet or speak with her over the phone. Driving around and talking to people that week proved priceless, because it gave her a better understanding of what executing her vision entailed. And she was happy to learn how friendly people were where she'd be living. Since she'd be driving to ranches to make client calls, learning how to get around the back roads of Montana would prove to be invaluable. Warm, friendly people were an unforeseen and happy bonus.

Client Outreach

At her current firm, Sarah was used to gaining new clients, earning their trust, and providing the services they needed, all of which would be relevant when working as a traveling ranch accountant. However, she wasn't trying to start a new business in Seattle but in faraway Montana. Being an outsider new to Montana and new to this type of business put her at a disadvantage. Some ranchers were happy to speak with her but made it clear they wouldn't change accountants. Many had worked with the same accounting firm for generations. Still, a handful of ranchers were receptive to learning more about her mobile service. Most of them would only make the long trek into town when absolutely necessary. If she could perform ranch calls and bring her services to the clients on their ranch, that would give her a competitive advantage. This trip helped her better understand the potential of her business model and how to start and grow her business, upgrading her knowledge base for this endeavor along the way.

Sarah was taking a big risk and had a lot to lose. No matter how prepared she was, bringing her vision to life required a leap of faith, so it was responsible for her to craft a backup plan. First, she made an arrangement with her current firm in Seattle to work remotely during the transition. Next, she researched firms in the Montana area that specialized in ranch accounting where she might be able to work if she was unable to get her own business venture off the ground quickly enough. She still wanted to pursue her fusioneering vision and dreamed of applying her trade while being out in the open country among the animals she so loved, but she needed to insulate herself in case things didn't go according to plan.

Sarah did a lot of independent research, but she was able to make such significant progress during her upgrade because of the success she had networking. She quickly learned that creating a successful business in Montana required having a healthy network of friends, colleagues, and clients. She couldn't do this alone. She needed help, and she was confident that she could get it.

Wherever Sarah went, almost everyone was friendly, open, and willing to help. When she would arrive in a town, having set up meetings and planned visits, the everyday people around town—those she met when out to eat or at the grocery store—proved surprisingly helpful in showing her the ropes. Those casual conversations gave her an overall understanding of the area and the culture that she never would have gotten by sitting home with her computer and phone. The people she met introduced her to new contacts, and she even met many of them when in town. Through all this networking, she learned how to position her business. Her mobile service not only gave her a chance to get out of the office and out on the ranch but also gave her a competitive advantage. She returned home after that trip to Montana even more excited about her vision than before she left.

Whether you learn on your own, from a stepping-stone position, or from a mentor, or you lean on the support of your network, it's important to understand that you don't need to rely on only one technique or learning style. Different approaches can be used when upgrading different skills. It might seem overwhelming at first, but you don't need to know all the answers right away. Sometimes you just have to dive in and figure out what works best for you. I learned the benefit of this during my upgrade.

CHAPTER 7

No Two Journeys Are the Same

When you're starting out, you may have an initial plan for pursuing your vision, but none of us can really know what's in store beforehand. We should anticipate having to be pragmatically flexible as each part of our journey unfolds.

I met Steve Elliott in the fall of 1993 during a break in my first-ever drawing class at the Loveland Academy of Fine Arts. Steve was a former ER doctor from Montana who had moved to Loveland to become a full-time oil painter. He later invited me to see his studio one afternoon. As soon as I walked in, I was hit with the smell of paint and turpentine. I saw the easel and all the canvases lying around and felt completely immersed in this creative world. It seemed like he lived such a romantic life, and I wanted to do the same.

After returning home from Sweden, where I had my life-altering experience visiting the traveling Leonardo da Vinci museum exhibit, I committed to the pursuit of my fusioneering vision. Construction finished on the art studio that I was going to lease in April 1994.

The day I moved in was the start of an exciting and romantic period of my life. And, yes, there was so much to do.

I first needed to design the floor plan to ensure I could fit in all the necessary equipment while still having enough space to efficiently work. In addition to the basics, such as a desk, bookcase, and filing cabinet, I needed space for a machine shop, computers, paints, an easel, canvases, a robot, and an electronics workbench and electronic controls cabinet. Fitting everything into the space proved to be a bit trickier than I initially assumed.

With the studio outfitted and the skills I needed to upgrade identified, I settled in and prepared myself for the years of upgrading that lay ahead. However, I didn't think about the time frame. I was so immersed in the journey that I enjoyed each day and lived in the moment. By fusing the things that I loved, I was living my dream.

Phase 1: Laying the Groundwork

Art was only one of several skills I needed to develop, and it required a steep learning curve. While I could study art history on my own, I knew that I couldn't teach myself how to paint, so I enrolled in art classes and was eager to learn.

Art Classes

Art classes provided me with the chance to immerse myself in this new creative world and meet other artists. The school was conveniently adjacent to my studio, so there was no commute involved; I just had to walk across the parking lot. The school offered three- and five-day workshops taught by visiting artists from around the country and ten-week classes taught by a local artist that met once a week.

I didn't need to wait long to experience the benefit. On the first day of my first oil painting class, the instructor said, "To be an artist, you don't just paint. You also have to study, take notes, visit galleries, read many books, and travel to museums." That simple statement had a profound impact on me. It influenced how I pursued my upgrade and the work I would later do with the robot. I will never forget those words.

Over the next six years, I took many drawing, painting, and sculpting classes. That might sound like a strictly fun pursuit, but if you're dedicated, classes can be intense. During that time, I studied with nineteen different instructors. They were all dedicated and well intentioned, but two stood out and had a profound impact on my learning. The first was David Leffel.

David Leffel is considered one of the greatest living American painters. Knowledgeable professional artists might consider him the best portrait and still life painter in the country. Not only is David a gifted artist, but he's also a gifted teacher. My skill as a painter advanced rapidly under his tutelage.

Put simply, David taught me how to paint. His approach resonated with me because he taught concepts, not rules. I could talk for hours about all the things I learned from David Leffel, but one of the most significant was the importance of the brushstroke. He said, "The brushstroke is the heart and soul of painting." Each stroke requires exquisite deliberation. It's made with three distinct motions: down, across, and up. There must be deliberate thought and intention behind each stroke. When David observed a student dabbing the canvas, he would always stop them. When you're dabbing paint onto the canvas, you're gambling with the outcome. Do that, and you will never win. Learning about the brushstroke influenced how I painted, making it clear to me that I needed the robot to have a wrist and control system capable of making those same exquisite brushstrokes.

From David, I also learned that before starting a painting I needed to distill my ideas down into a single concept that would drive every artistic decision I made for that particular work of art.

Paul's oil painting from art class, where he learned the lifelong lesson that the brushstroke is the heart and soul of painting

This was essential because if, during the process, I ever had an artistic question, like about a compositional design element, I could refer back to that overreaching umbrella concept.

I was fortunate to take a one-week workshop with David every October for the next six years, but art classes weren't all I was doing. While upgrading my skills in art, I simultaneously started to upgrade the skills required to build the robot. Because of the complexity and size of the task ahead of me, the best way for me to learn was to just start building and see where it would lead me. With my degree in electrical engineering, combined with my background at HP Labs and in an Air Force research lab, at this point I just had to learn the rest by doing. I knew there was a long road ahead, fraught with problems; I just didn't know what those problems would be yet. Through it all, I followed my enthusiasm each day.

Machine Shop

I knew ahead of time that I'd need my own machine shop to build the custom parts for the robot. I purchased a brand-new industrial mill, and my machinist friend Bob Morgan helped me track down a used lathe in Denver that I could refurbish. It was quite a sight watching the delivery men try to carefully load the large equipment through the sliding back door of my studio with a forklift. Unlike the standard 240 volts required to run machines like washers and dryers, both pieces of equipment required 360-volt, three-phase industrial power. That's one reason I had arranged with the owner of my unit to have extra utility power installed while it was under construction.

I already had some machine shop experience. I took a vo-tech class back in 1980 while working at HP, and I set up a small machine shop in my garage when building my first robot. That provided me with a basic understanding of how to work with metal. However, there is only so much you can learn about metalwork in ten evenings, so I searched for as many VHS tapes on metalworking as I could find, but back then, there weren't that many available.

These machines were very dangerous, so I needed to learn how to be extremely careful and pay close attention to detail. With time and care, I improved my skills enough to design and make all the custom parts I needed. I didn't need to become a master machinist; I only needed to gain a certain level of proficiency. Had I not reached that skill level, I would not have been able to build the robot.

I had always enjoyed building things with my hands, so it was no surprise that I had so much fun working in that machine shop. I'd often get lost within myself because it's so enjoyable and empowering once you develop a certain level of skill in a new domain.

Adept Technology

When I was a venture capitalist, I was fortunate to be a first-round investor in Adept Technology, a robotics startup company in San Jose, California. They went on to become the largest American robot company. As a member of the corporate board of directors, I must have traveled back and forth to San Jose more than a hundred times. Since I was familiar with their business and robotics, it was natural for me to use their advanced, world-class robotics computer for my robot. In 1994, I reached out to Brian Carlisle, the CEO and founder, to see if I could attend their two-week industrial customer training class held at their headquarters. There, I could learn the basics of robotics, the robotic work cell, their controller, and proprietary robotic programming language.

The attendees were factory engineers from around the country who were there because their companies wanted to use or improve their automation with robotics. You could tell these engineers were under pressure and singularly focused. I was there for a completely different reason. In time, my instructors learned of my relationship with Adept, but I certainly didn't want any special attention.

Paul in his machine shop, immersed in the joys of working with his lathe and mill

I learned a lot in two weeks, and that class helped me develop a robotics foundation. The documentation from that class now fills two full bookshelves in my studio. There was so much of it that I couldn't bring it on the plane with me; I had to ship it home. I'm glad I did, because I frequently refer to those manuals and have dog-eared many pages over the years.

After that class, I bought a beautiful, high-end Adept robot controller that was probably the most advanced in the world at the time. In the robotic world, these computers are called *controllers* because they must operate in real time, be able to process multiple programs concurrently, and manage all the operations of the robotic work cell.

Steel Structure

The ten-by-ten-foot steel structure I intended to build would resemble a freestanding wall. It was needed to support the gantry-style robot, designed to move along the *x*-, *y*-, and *z*-axes with a robotic

Ever since he was a young child, Paul always liked making things with his hands.

wrist at the end of the z-axis to hold the paintbrush. I initially built a wooden frame out of two-by-fours, so I could envision the robot and the robotic work cell space.

The robot carriage weighed hundreds of pounds and needed to move smoothly in multiple directions. The steel structure needed to be strong and rigid to carry the load and avoid vibration, so this required a strong and rigid design. Back then, computer-aided design (CAD) software was very expensive. Luckily, my machinist friend had a much cheaper student version I could use. After purchasing a large printer, I first had to learn how to use the software and then how to make detailed engineering drawing specifications for the welded structure that, when assembled, would weigh close to two thousand pounds.

With my drawings complete, I brought them to three firms in Denver to bid on the project. The first two didn't want to touch it, but the third firm agreed. Once the structure was built, the workers arrived at the studio with heavy equipment to lift everything into place and assemble it. The installation was smooth. They did an excellent job. My only regret is that I didn't ask them to spray-paint the structure as well, but I was trying to save money. It turned into a mess with paint mist in the air and plastic sheets hanging throughout the studio. But once I had it painted, it felt good seeing the structure standing there in the studio. At this stage, it was just an empty wall. There was no robot or even the hint of one yet.

Building the Carriage

With the steel structure in place, I worked on both the fixed and moving parts of the carriage system. That involved building the sliding rail systems, timing belts, and cable carriers (like you'd see in a car wash) and mounting the motors and gearing systems so the robot could move up, down, left, and right across the canvas. I would eventually use flat magnets or masking tape to mount the canvas to the wall.

Motors and Controls

Once the motors were bolted and mounted in place, they needed to be connected to a control system with cabling to give them power. Each motor and gear assembly had an encoder for rotational positional feedback to the robotic controller. The robot's controller, the controls, power amps for the motors, and all the other electronics were installed in a six-foot-tall electronic cabinet standing adjacent to the robot.

Electronics

My electrical engineering and computer science background (and my time at HP Labs) gave me a solid foundation in electronics.

The first steps, with the future unknowable, but full of potential

This was one of my most developed skills and required the least on-the-job training, but there was still a learning curve, so I needed to further develop these skills. While I may have been familiar with electronics, I knew nothing about the electronics needed to drive and control industrial motors and gears.

If the goal was to build a robot that could make beautiful brushstrokes, the robotic wrist had to mimic the movements of a human wrist. In addition to the wrist motors, gearing, and optical encoders, it would need a sophisticated control system and computer to run it all.

Another aspect of the electronics and control system, which took considerable time to design and build, was a paint-level sensor for the brush. As you paint, especially after dozens or hundreds of brushstrokes for one paint color, the paint level goes down in the jar. In order to make accurate and exquisitely controlled brushstrokes, the robotic controller needs to sense that exact level of paint for each dip of the brush into the paint. Eventually, with the accuracy of the robot's vertical movement of the wrist assembly

The early days for Paul and Dulcinea, with a challenging pathway ahead

and my circuit design, I could detect the paint level to about a fifth of a millimeter, or around one-hundredth of an inch. David Leffel would have liked that.

I was making progress. It was exciting to see the robot taking form, but there was so much left to do that I couldn't relax.

Hooking Everything Up

Next up was routing all the power and control cabling from the robot's seven servo motors through multiple cable carriers mounted on the steel structure. More than fifty feet of cable winds up, around, and down to the electronic cabinet and Adept's controller. There were other sensors used in the robotic work cell that needed power too, and their wiring also routed back to the cabinet.

Once all the connections were completed, the controller still had no knowledge of what it was connected to or of the robot. I had to carefully configure the controller's operating system for my particular hardware configuration, and set of motors, controls, and

Deep inside the six-foot-tall electronic control cabinet

I/O (input–output) systems. The stack of recorded documentation for this requires dozens of pages. What I thought might take weeks turned into months.

Unanticipated Problems

The robot was coming together, and I had learned a tremendous amount about motors and gears, carriage systems, operating systems, I/O control systems, and robotic coding software. At first, I'd write and run small test programs, so the robot would move from one designated point to another before attempting more difficult tasks. After all this work and time, it was exciting yet nerve-racking watching the robot finally move. Luckily, it all worked well. You could hear my sigh of relief, at least for a little while.

During one run, as the robot traveled from left to right along the x-axis carriage system, the entire system crashed. The computer error message read, "X-axis out of range." How could that be? It was sitting right there in the middle of the structure.

Adept's CEO told me that if I ever got into trouble and needed assistance, to call Glenn Helmes, from Cincinnati. Glenn visited factories all over the world as a troubleshooter, helping companies solve robotic and automation manufacturing problems. Sometimes he'd be on location for months at a time. He reminded me of the character Paladin from the old Western television show *Have Gun Will Travel.*

When his schedule freed up, Glenn came to Loveland to help me out. He first wanted to examine the operating system controls I had in place, which included tuning the operating performance controls for all the motors. There were seven motors in total that would eventually work in harmony to deliver those exquisite brushstrokes that I wanted. Once all the operations were tuned to his satisfaction, we could address why the system crashed. Watching Glenn work was amazing and allowed me to relax, at least momentarily.

Some of the cabling was fifty feet long, and even with insulation, that cabling acts like a giant antenna transmitting electromagnetic interference (electrical noise). That noise had tricked the controller and caused the system to crash. The electrical interference was so bad it would completely disrupt the television reception of my artist friend three doors down. For those interested, $V = L \times \mathrm{d}i/\mathrm{d}t$. Voltage is proportional to the length of cable multiplied by the change of current and divided by the change in time. In lay terms, with my giant fifty-foot-long antenna, bursts of huge current surges to drive large motors could wreak havoc.

In addition to the electromagnetic interference, trust me when I say that every journey will have its unforeseen obstacles, large and small. The first wrist I built in the machine shop used standard, off-the-shelf motors. The performance, accuracy, and smoothness I needed for those desired brushstrokes wasn't satisfactory with that first design. Instead, I had to totally redesign and build a new wrist, this time incorporating expensive, state-of-the-art servomotors and zero-backlash gearing systems.

One Final Hurdle

I had one technical problem to solve before the robot and I were ready to paint, and it was a big one.

A good artist knows that you must carefully control the amount of paint on the brush. You can't have half an inch of paint on your brush if you only need to make a slight highlight. So if some strokes require the robot to dip the brush a millimeter into the paint and other strokes require dipping the brush two or more millimeters, how would the robot know the level of paint in each jar, and how far to dip the brush? What makes this even more complex is that the paint is thick and its surface in the jar is not flat. Not all jars have the same level of paint after they are mixed, and the paint level will go down as more brushstrokes use up the paint in the jar. I needed to develop a paint-level sensor that took every factor into consideration.

This was an extremely difficult problem. I asked a close family friend who was an aerospace design engineer, and he couldn't solve it. It took a lot of time and intense research into my electronic analog circuit design books. I also received a valuable suggestion from an engineering friend I knew from the gym. Eventually, I created an elegant electronic circuit that uses calculus to accurately sense the varying levels of paint to within a quarter of a millimeter in any given jar. That's no small feat; there is no other painting robot in the world that I am aware of that can sense its level of paint. David Leffel would have liked that.

Phase 2: Refining the Vision

As the robot neared completion in 2000, the Loveland art school closed. However, that wasn't the end of my art upgrade. My last class was with the second instructor who would also significantly impact my upgrade and my life.

After Glenn Vilppu graduated from CalArts in Santa Clarita, near Los Angeles, he taught animators at Walt Disney Studios how to draw. More than six decades later, well into his eighties, he's still teaching drawing classes and spends many weeks each summer teaching weeklong classes in various countries throughout Europe.

When I first walked into Glenn's class in Loveland, there were only six other students. I was surprised to learn the woman sitting next to me at the drawing table had come all the way from Los Angeles. She told me there was never any room in his classes in L.A.

When the class broke for lunch each day at noon, I'd walk over to my studio. On Friday, the last day of class, a woman asked if she could come see the studio. When Glenn heard where we were going, he asked to come along too. I agreed, and as we walked over, I was nervous about what he would think of my oil paintings and the robot I was building.

When he entered the studio and looked around, I could tell he was thrilled with the robot and what I was trying to create. Glenn was hard of hearing and hadn't yet gotten his cochlear implants, so I spent the rest of the lunch hour writing out my answers to his many questions on a yellow legal pad. The time flew by, and he never ended up eating lunch.

Early the next morning, after our class had ended and everyone had traveled home, I was at work in the studio when I heard a soft knock on the door. It was Glenn and his wife, Eleanor. I invited them inside and spent the entire morning again answering his questions by writing on my pad. The conversation became so involved that they missed an appointment they had later that day. That was the fortuitous beginning of a wonderful friendship.

As I said, while the school may have closed in 2000, that wasn't the end of my education. In some ways, it was only the beginning. What I would learn about art over the next twenty-plus years made so much of what I have accomplished to date possible. With art—or any other passion, really—you always want to grow. That's the challenge, excitement, and reward for a passion. And nothing helped me do that as much as studying the masters.

Roberta and Henry were a couple who organized study trips to Europe for a group of twelve to fifteen artists, along with a featured artist, typically Glenn. They organized only one trip a year, usually to a different country, and typically for twelve days. And they always made sure to arrange a fascinating travel itinerary.

My first trip with the group was to Italy in 2002. We started in the quiet region of Lucca and ended up in Venice. Each morning in Lucca, before setting out for the day, we'd gather around Glenn, who would use his sketchbook, ink, and sometimes watercolors to give a mini art and drawing lecture. The rest of the day unfolded like an adventure. We'd stop somewhere scenic, unfold our small stools, take out our field sketch kits, and try to capture a scene while applying concepts we had learned that morning or earlier in the trip. Glenn's role as such a generous and kind teacher is what made this artistic immersion so enjoyable.

During another trip to Florence, we stayed near the famous Ponte Vecchio bridge. Much like Venice, it was all so romantic. I learned a lot about sketching, but it was Glenn's lectures on art history and art concepts—such as composition—delivered while standing right in front of the original masterpieces, that vividly brought the lessons to life. When viewing a painting in a museum, we'd gather around Glenn as he talked about the piece and the artist. Sometimes he would spend thirty minutes discussing various artistic and compositional concepts. He'd then often sit on a nearby museum bench and demonstrate an artistic concept in his sketchbook, as we gathered around to look over his shoulder.

Like David Leffel, Glenn taught the importance of establishing a concept for each new painting that drives every artistic decision you make. He referred to it as "the gesture." No matter what you're trying to paint, the essence of that scene (the gesture) needs to be captured.

This lesson was instilled in me during another trip to Tuscany. It was late afternoon in the foothills, and our art group was sketching

Paul's ink-and-watercolor Tuscany castle

outside our hilltop villa when dark clouds rolled in. I was proud of the ink and watercolor sketch I had made of a castle sitting on top of a neighboring hill. I had even captured the dark clouds. But when Glenn inspected my work, he critically said that I had failed to capture the gesture. That was all he said, but it was enough. The essence of the scene required the viewer's eye to rise up the steep side of the craggy hill to the medieval castle on top. Simply changing the placement of the castle from the middle of my paper to the top would make a significant difference. That was a lesson that stuck with me. Today, I make sure to succinctly establish and capture the overriding concept, or gesture, before I begin each new painting with Dulcinea.

During another memorable trip, we were in the National Gallery in London, which remains one of my favorite art museums. I had been there before and had already heard Glenn's mini lecture, so I went to view a painting by Michelangelo Merisi da Caravaggio in an adjacent room. Caravaggio is one of the heavyweights from the 1500s. I was familiar with his work but not this piece, *The Taking of Christ*. The painting depicts Judas and the Roman soldiers trying to take Christ from the Garden of Gethsemane. It's large, dark, and overwhelming. Google images are much brighter than the painting itself. While gazing at it for a long time, I couldn't understand what the artist was trying to capture.

Over the years, Glenn repeatedly taught us that to truly understand an artist's intentions, you should make a quick sketch of the composition in your sketchbook to capture the compositional forms and movement of your eye within the painting. I'd seen him do this many times, magically uncovering layers of artistic design and nuance in a painting. Movement, along with other considerations—such as subject matter, draftsmanship, values, color, texture, and brushwork—entertain our eye, sometimes without us fully understanding why.

Right there in the National Gallery, while I could still hear Glenn lecturing in the adjacent room, that's exactly what I did. I took out my sketchbook and tried to capture the compositional design and movement in Caravaggio's masterpiece. These sketches aren't big, typically four by six inches. Creating one only took two or three minutes. However, when finished, I still didn't comprehend Caravaggio's intention and compositional design. So I started over and made a second sketch. And a third. It wasn't until the fifth sketch that I got it. There it was, buried in the darkness of the painting! The soft glimmer of light subtly reflected off the soldiers' armor and helmets, dividing the painting along the lines of the golden mean, and directing the eye to Judas and Christ on the far left.

Moments like that are thrilling, and during my nine trips to Europe with Glenn, I was fortunate to experience a number of similar *aha* moments. It was such an amazing experience to stand

Some of Paul's small notebooks while traveling with Glenn in Europe (top)
Paul's travel ink and watercolor sketch kit (bottom)

in front of masterpieces in major art museums and have Glenn by my side, serving as my tutor. Nothing compared to that learning experience.

I consider those lessons I've learned from both Glenn Vilppu and David Leffel as priceless gifts for which I am forever grateful. Whether it's the significance of the brushstroke or the importance of concept when developing a new piece of art, they are always on my mind whenever I work on a new painting.

A New Direction

My original vision to fuse the theoretical with the aesthetic was conceived while I was in business school. Back then, I wanted to build a business using robots that turned photographs into paintings for customers. However, after spending years taking art classes and visiting museums in Europe, I fell in love with the pure creative process and learned to appreciate the beauty of original artwork. I don't know if I'd consider myself a talented artist, but I developed a deep respect for the creative process. Given that, where was the artistic creativity in copying a photograph? While electromechanically interesting, my original idea had lost its appeal.

Consider the greats, from Leonardo and Michelangelo during the Renaissance to El Greco and Tintoretto during the Mannerist period, Caravaggio during the late Mannerist period, Bernini in the Baroque period, impressionists like Monet and Cezanne, postimpressionists like van Gogh, and even artists in the 1950s New York School like Franz Kline, Clyfford Still, and Robert Motherwell. None of them ever copied anything! They were all pioneers. Every one of the greats was always striving and pushing themselves to create something unique. They were driven to explore possibilities and challenge themselves. That's how they broke new ground to become great. That's what excited them. And that's what excited me! That's what I wanted to do. I wanted to strive to create individual masterpieces, breaking new ground with my robot. Fusioneers naturally want to keep evolving. It's natural for them because they're living their dream, and that dream may shift as they grow, learn, and naturally expand their capabilities and vision.

From this, I developed two rules. First, there would be no copying of photographs or using someone's pixel data. Every piece of art the robot created would be an original work. The second rule was to never retouch a painting when it was completed by the robot. I'd get what I got, and that was it.

What Do I Paint?

With the robot finally built and running smoothly, I needed to figure out what we were going to paint. Since I wasn't copying photographs, where would the art come from, you might wonder? That's a great question! That's where imagination, curiosity, and then layers of coding are used to create the structure of the painting that the robot will eventually paint. This began a fascinating journey that involved many technical approaches and years of learning. It continues to evolve and will do so indefinitely.

I was originally exposed to programming back in high school in 1967. I was part of a small group of students selected from local high schools to attend a programming class that summer at San Jose State. We used punch cards at the time, and things hadn't changed much the following year when I enrolled in a freshman programming class at Berkeley. Once we typed up and submitted a stack of IBM punch cards for our class homework assignment, the turnaround time was slow and often took hours. We'd often have to visit the campus computing center in the middle of the night to get the results and see if our programming assignment ran successfully. The whole process created a sense of dread because, if we had made even just a single mistake or typo, we'd have to start the cycle all over again.

When I set out to upgrade my coding skills thirty years later in the late 1990s, a lot had changed. Artificial intelligence was a hot topic at the time, and I saw a lot of promising possibilities, but how could I learn about AI? Google didn't exist, Amazon was still small, and there weren't many AI books at Barnes and Noble. Still, I managed to track down two books that both later became classics: *Paradigms of Artificial Intelligence Programming: Case Studies in Common Lisp* by Peter Norvig and *Artificial Intelligence: A Modern Approach* by Stuart Russell and Peter Norvig. Both used snippets of a high-level programming language called Lisp to illustrate various AI concepts and techniques. Lisp became my programming language of choice, which over time proved to be a fortuitous decision.

I needed to have an in-depth mastery of Lisp, and the learning curve was steep. I attended a three-day Lisp programming class in San Francisco and gained some knowledge, but the material was too advanced. Most everyone else in that class was beyond me. However, over time, I built up a respectable library of books on Lisp, high-level coding techniques, and AI. I had a deep desire to learn, and my curiosity provided all the motivation I needed to reach the necessary levels of proficiency.

By its very nature, everyone's journey will be unique unto themselves as it unfolds. But the amazing thing I learned, and what all might share, is that when pursuing your vision, you'll have sustaining enthusiasm and energy. And even though it may not always be easy or pleasant, you're living your dream with a growing sense of fulfillment. You're living your reason for being, as you were meant to live.

Paul lost in that wonderful state of flow

PART 3

START

Valentin Okorokov was my extremely gifted Russian sculpture teacher at the Loveland Academy of Fine Arts. Before fleeing Moscow during the Cold War, his bronze monuments were in eleven museums in the Soviet Union. Seeking freedom, he left all his possessions behind and snuck out of the country with only a satchel of sculpting tools. His wife, Olga, would later join him.

Sculpting came surprisingly easy to me. While it might have had something to do with some of my innate intelligences (visual and kinesthetic), with Valentin's added tutelage, my hands just knew what to do. I enjoyed it, and I got to know Valentin. One evening, while I was having dinner in his home, he explained to me that he didn't sculpt because he wanted to; he sculpted because he had to.

That visceral drive is what's possible when you find your true calling. It's what I experienced once I set out on my journey. It may have taken a long time for my upgrade to come together, but I loved every minute of it. I was like a kid playing with Tinker Toys. There was no sacrifice involved because there was nothing else that I would rather be doing. This was in my blood. I didn't have to force any of it, because I wanted to do it. When you experience this feeling, you know you're on the right path.

Your upgrade never ends because you never stop learning, and that's a good thing. As we will discuss, during this journey you will often have to circle back to upgrade various skills or acquire new ones as your vision evolves and new obstacles present themselves. Since this process is fluid, it can be difficult for some to identify when they should transition out of the upgrade phase and begin the start phase.

For some people, this isn't a difficult decision. They know that if they start fusing only to learn they aren't ready, they can easily return to upgrade. However, if you're starting a business or pursuing a vision that requires a major life change or a certain investment of time and money, prematurely starting the fusioneering process might result in adverse consequences. So how do you know when the time is right?

When working as a venture capitalist, I met with hundreds of entrepreneurs and reviewed even more business plans, but we only invested in two or three companies per year. That required us to make difficult decisions when whittling down our vast list. My partner and I made sure we did our due diligence and thoroughly researched each business proposal and the team involved. A final decision would always require good business judgment. Feeling like something was missing, however, I did some research on what makes a good decision. There is a lot written on this topic, but it all boils down to a simple concept that is quite easy to apply: Before you make a final decision, both your head and your stomach need to be in agreement.

Do you *think* it's the right time to move forward? Do you *feel* it's the right time to move forward? Those are two very different questions, and if the answer isn't yes to both, it's probably not the best time for you to proceed to start. It doesn't mean that you won't succeed if both aren't in agreement. It just means that you put yourself in the best position to succeed when what you think and feel are in alignment.

You've worked hard to nurture and cultivate your dream, and you now have the opportunity to start making it a reality. This section of your journey is a milestone and a clear dividing line in the process. While the previous path markers were about preparation, now we begin the execution phase. This is when you start fusing. You'll use the skill sets you upgraded to help bring your vision to life.

There are two ways to approach this phase: an immediate start and a gradual start. Each one is self-explanatory. Some people dive right in and figure things out as they go. Others require a gradual start as they ease their way into it. Determining the right approach depends entirely upon your vision and your circumstances. When finances are involved, and you're trying to make a living, a gradual start is an excellent way to ensure you have the proper safety net. For those who don't have as much to lose or have turned to fusioneering to reconnect with their passion, it might be best for them to jump right in.

Having already upgraded the necessary skills to attain the required level of proficiency, you've learned the importance of making adjustments along the way. That will continue through this phase because you still don't know all there is to know. That means obstacles should be expected, and problems will arise. We'll discuss various problem-solving techniques and tools to help you overcome those obstacles while on your journey. There will be times when you need to take risks, and armed with a knowledge of your domain and the ability to work through difficult problems, you have a much higher chance of success.

This phase is exciting and filled with moments of apprehension at the same time. If you are starting a business, you might have a lot at stake, so recognizing when to adjust your plan is more important than ever. Adjustments will often be necessary, and sometimes they require adding an additional leg to your stool. That might mean returning to the upgrade phase to become proficient in an entirely new set of skills. You might be able to do this while still pursuing your vision, or you might have to circle back. Every situation is different, so you must determine what approach is appropriate for your vision.

While on this journey, it's important not to lose sight of the traits and behaviors that got you this far. You must remain curious, creative, and driven. You want to keep learning about your domains and honing your skill sets; that should never end. If you've already become autotelic, this should come naturally. You will have learned to thrive on challenges, developed dogged persistence when trying to overcome obstacles, and most important, won't be waiting to find enjoyment until the end of the process because, when you're autotelic, you already feel that sense of accomplishment and fulfillment. You will encounter new challenges—that's to be expected—but armed with a new set of tools, many of those challenges can result in significant breakthroughs that you might not have thought possible.

CHAPTER 8

Sharpen Your Problem-Solving Skills

When I was ready to start, I couldn't have been more euphoric, and you should be too! You've come an incredibly long way. You've done your homework, studied your domains, and improved your skill sets. That will get you off on the right foot and put you in the best position to succeed. However, no matter how well you prepare, not everything will go according to plan. When you encounter problems, there is no one-size-fits-all solution. Each problem is unique and may require a different approach. What makes some problems particularly difficult to solve is that you can't predict when and where they will occur. So having some proven problem-solving techniques at your disposal can prevent you from getting discouraged. You want to remain on

Paul drawing on whiteboard

the path forward, and this chapter focuses on three powerful techniques you can apply when you reach a critical juncture and need to solve a problem: relying on first principles, prioritized execution, and finding your flow.

First Principles

What often prevents us from solving a problem is our assumption about the root cause and our misunderstanding of how certain things actually work. Other times, we might not understand the very nature of the problem. One way to overcome these issues is a problem-solving method called *first principles*. It involves deconstructing the problem and reconstructing the solution from the ground up. It's about looking at the individual components that make up the whole, not just the whole. This helps you gain a brand-new perspective that can open up a world of new possibilities.

This valuable tool isn't anything new; it goes back thousands of years. Aristotle called first principles "the first basis from which a thing is known." By breaking the problem down to its essential building blocks and by understanding what is known and unknown about those parts, you can better understand the whole. That puts you in a better position to identify and solve the problem. It's like erasing the blackboard and starting over so you aren't burdened by what has been done before. You are literally going back to the drawing board.

Over the years, I've modified this process and found the following seven steps work best for me. I've relied on this technique when an aspect of a new painting just didn't feel right or when trying to figure out a difficult coding issue. I once spent two long days solving a single coding bug, and it would have taken me much longer had I not followed these steps. Even then, I still had to loop back through these steps several times. Besides addressing problems, this technique can provide entirely new insights and solutions. It can also help you gain confidence as you move forward. First-principles thinking has proved invaluable for me, and it's a simple concept to understand. Here's how it works.

Step 1: State the Goal or Problem

Come up with a statement that best encapsulates the problem or your goal. Get it down on paper. The clearer and more concise, the better. The more detail you can provide, the easier the next step becomes.

Step 2: Break the Problem Down into Its Most Basic Parts

Next, deconstruct that statement by breaking it down into its most basic parts. Think of how a car works. It's not just one piece of equipment. It's a complex machine consisting of thousands of moving parts. If your car suddenly stops running, the mechanic doesn't look at the car as a whole and expect to solve the problem. The mechanic must first pinpoint the source of the fault, and that is done by identifying the problem and breaking down its various parts. It's a waste of time to examine the engine and the tires if you've determined the problem is electrical. However, that still doesn't give you the answer you need. You must break those electrical parts down further. Is it the battery, alternator, starter, or ignition system? If it is the ignition system, you then need to examine the spark plugs, ignition wires, coils, and so forth. On and on it goes, and the mechanic must keep breaking down the problem until the most basic parts are identified.

You don't need a solution yet, and you don't want to jump to conclusions. You just want to list all the possible components linked to your problem or goal.

Step 3: List All of the Facts

In this step, you want to determine what is absolutely true (what Aristotle described as "known by nature and timeless") about each part. This is when you separate facts from assumptions. This can be more difficult than it seems on the surface because the more you think about the components of a problem, the more you might realize that some of what you believe to be facts are actually assumptions.

Step 4: List All of Your Assumptions

We sometimes don't see assumptions as assumptions; we believe them to be true, which prevents us from challenging those ideas. We often take for granted what we "know," or assume the way we typically do things is the right or only way to do things. However, our understanding of the world doesn't always match how the world operates. Sometimes our assumptions might be the source of our problem. If we don't ask these questions and separate our assumptions from facts, we might never identify the true source of the problem.

Here's an example of false assumptions. Consider the following maze and look for all the different ways you can get from one side to the other.

How many paths did you discover? Did it ever cross your mind not to go through the maze the traditional way? Why not go around the side of the maze? How about over the top? If that did occur to you, congratulations, because that's a sign that you will be very good at this type of thinking. If not, don't worry; most people don't think like that immediately. We've been doing these types of mazes for most of our lives, and we always knew that we couldn't just go around the side or over the top because those were the rules. Since it was never an option, we don't naturally think to do that. It's counterintuitive, and that's what can be challenging about first-principles thinking. That's where the next step comes in.

Step 5: Ask Lots of Questions

The more you question the facts and assumptions, the easier it will be to clearly divide them into two distinct lists. Most likely, your vision fuses existing domains and well-established ways of doing things. You're naturally building on what has worked in the past and what someone else has done before. It's easy to assume that it's the right or only way to do things. It may be the best way, but how can you know for sure if you don't look closely, break it down, and ask questions?

For this exercise, don't take what you think you know for granted, no matter how simple or obvious it may seem. Question and challenge what you know about every single part of your problem. Dig into the basic building blocks; can they be divided even further? Be honest about your assumptions and what you might not know or understand. Ask yourself why things are the way they are, but don't stop there and *only* focus on what's been done before. Ask driving, exploratory questions not even related to your list of facts and assumptions. Sometimes the answers to those questions are the most valuable. Take your time, really push yourself to reach out, and ask probing, challenging questions.

Step 6: Create One or More Hypotheses

This is the time to brainstorm new solutions to problems and come up with new ways to approach your goals. Don't expect to find any solutions right away. See where those questions lead you. Develop as many new hypotheses as possible, because they can lead to valuable insights. Take your time to delve deeply into this entire process. There might be a hidden gem waiting for you.

Step 7: Reconstruct and Evaluate

Once you have one or more hypotheses, pick your favorite and test it. See how it turns out before moving on to the next hypothesis.

You might not find a solution right away, so loop back through the steps if necessary. When you find the solution you need, it's like finding a gold nugget. It will ring true.

Elon Musk is a big proponent of first-principles thinking. He may be a polarizing figure, but it's difficult to deny the success he has achieved using this method. He often refers to it as approaching problems from a physics framework and not reasoning by analogy or copying what others have done. It's how Tesla developed less expensive batteries and how SpaceX decided to use reusable rockets. Instead of simply doing what had been done before and relying on old technology, Musk disregarded all previous assumptions and came to new conclusions that fit each of his company's needs.

There are variations of this concept that can be helpful when trying to solve a problem. In the 1970s, Toyota implemented what has become known as the five whys technique when developing its manufacturing process. This simple technique is intended to help you find the root cause of a problem by first asking, "Why did this problem occur?" Don't settle for that first answer. Ask why and keep asking why after each answer until you get to the source. The number of times you have to ask the question isn't important. You might find the answer after two questions, or it might take seven. When your answer is "I don't know," you've reached a useful starting point. It's about breaking the problem down to its root cause, so you can build it back up. Similar to first principles, the five whys approach forces you to break from conventional thinking and dig deeper to question what you think you know.

These techniques can be applied to any part of life and are crucial to fusioneering. When faced with a problem, break it down into its most basic parts. Determine facts from assumptions, and then reason upward until you come to a new solution. This is an invaluable tool for solving one problem, but what happens when you feel overwhelmed and faced with multiple problems simultaneously?

Prioritize and Execute

In the phenomenal book *Extreme Ownership*, authors Jocko Willink and Leif Babin deconstruct a law of combat called "prioritize and execute." Babin tells the story of leading a SEAL platoon deep into an area of Ramadi, Iraq, held by enemy insurgents. The mission was to disrupt the insurgent safe haven and kill as many enemy fighters as possible to decrease their ability to attack nearby Marine outposts.

Once they were in enemy territory, the team hunkered down in an apartment building that gave them a clear tactical advantage and a commanding view of the location. Surrounded by enemy troops, they had to hold their position as they endured an onslaught of machine gun fire and rocket-propelled grenades from all directions. They were unable to call for outside help, since it would put those rescuing soldiers at risk. Periods of intense violence were followed by periods of calm. This went on throughout the day.

The attacks ended at sundown. Having achieved their main objectives, the SEAL team prepared to leave through the only way in and out of the building. That's when they spotted an IED (improvised explosive device) placed just outside that doorway by the insurgents. They were unable to exit or scale down the building from the windows or roof because it would place them in harm's way. Their only option was to sledgehammer an opening through a thick concrete wall so they could safely exit to an adjoining rooftop.

They couldn't leave the live IED behind, because it would put future American and Iraqi soldiers at risk. So before departing, they set a charge on a timer that would allow them to get safely away from the building before it detonated. Once through the hole and out on the rooftop, the platoon was exposed and vulnerable to insurgent fighters, who were already aware of their location.

Suddenly, a SEAL crashed through the weakened roof and hit the concrete twenty feet below. The team was unable to communicate with him, and there was an iron gate preventing them from descending the only stairway leading to the ground level. Meanwhile, the timer they had set to blow the IED was ticking, and they only had a few minutes before it would detonate. There was no time to waste.

Faced with a dilemma, and numerous existential problems, Babin was forced to *prioritize and execute*. He took a step back to distance himself from his immediate emotional reaction. He then had to determine the team's greatest priority. They would focus on that priority until it was satisfactorily addressed and then turn their attention to the next priority. He could not afford to be overwhelmed. His men's lives were at stake. He had to "relax, look around, and make the call."

Priority 1

He called out, "Set security!" As much as they wanted to help their wounded man, they first needed to occupy the strongest tactical position possible to defend themselves. That required putting men in key covering positions to protect themselves from insurgents who could fire upon them at any time.

Priority 2

He called out, "Breacher up!" That meant they needed to break through that locked iron gate.

Priority 3

Then, he ordered, "Head count!" They had to ensure every man was accounted for prior to descending the stairs and exiting the building.

Priority 4

"Move out!" They recovered the injured man, set security on the street, and exited the building. They all made it to a safe distance by the time the IED detonated.

Having been trained to prioritize and execute, the entire team was able to work together when stepping beyond their comfort zone to assess problems and make critical decisions under pressure. They understood that if they tried to solve every problem simultaneously, none of them would be solved. Even when faced with a situation where everything was a priority, they were forced to prioritize.

Babin's narration of this dramatic scenario left an indelible impression on me. However, this isn't a technique reserved only for combat. Prioritize and execute (P&E, as I've come to call it) can be applied in all situations and in all walks of life. By its very nature, your fusioneering journey is about combining things. Even when not facing a life-and-death wartime scenario, as a fusioneer you will find many things you'll want or need to do and many problems to solve.

Whether they are minor annoyances or complex problems, they can quickly compound and snowball. When faced with multiple action items on your to-do list or unexpected challenges, it's natural to try and tackle them all at once. However, that spreads your energy, attention, and resources thin, making it difficult to resolve any of those items. Always start with the understanding that you can't address every problem all at once. That doesn't mean those other priorities aren't important. It means you must focus your resources and energy on the most pressing priority first.

How do you know which priority is the most pressing? When you consider the stakes and time frames for each, it becomes much easier to arrange those problems in order of priority. You don't need to ignore or pull all your resources from other priorities to address your top priority. You simply give that first priority all of the resources required to solve the problem. It's ideal if you can do that without exacerbating other problems or creating new ones, but depending on the situation, that might be unavoidable. Once the first problem is satisfactorily addressed, you can move on to the next problem or action item.

Prioritize and execute may sound like a simple, commonsense approach to problem solving. You "relax, look around, and make a call." But it's that first part, *relax*, that is often the hardest for some. When faced with problems, people can quickly become overwhelmed and emotional. And we don't typically make the best decisions when we're emotional. For this technique to be most effective, Willink speaks about the power of knowing how and when to detach, so you can view the situation differently and gain new perspectives.

Circumstances might determine the best way to detach. If you're working with a group of people, try physically moving your body back just a bit or to a different location. Even if you are working alone on your computer, getting up and changing your environment is a good way to detach. Once you've stepped away, take a deep breath, relax your body, and try to calm down before deciding. If you don't need to make an immediate decision, take your time and then gather your thoughts. Sleep on it if necessary. The time frame required for you to detach may vary. This is the exact reason it's advised not to respond to emails when you're upset. It's always better to take time to gather your thoughts. That advice is just another form of detaching. It's all about preventing you from making irrational emotional decisions.

Knowing when to detach can be more difficult if you're not used to doing it because you haven't yet identified when you are and when you aren't detached. It's like the boiling frog apologue. Put a frog in a pot of already boiling water, and it will immediately jump out, but if the frog is placed in a pan of room-temperature water that is slowly brought to a boil, it won't identify the threat before it's too late and it boils to death. Problems creep up on us, and we can become flustered and frustrated before we identify the state we're in.

Just because you take a step away and say you're detached doesn't mean that you are no longer emotionally involved. You need to be honest in your assessment of the situation. If you aren't detached and able to see the situation from a new perspective, you might make impulsive decisions. You might not properly prioritize and execute, making the problem worse. Detachment requires self-awareness. The more you use detaching, the more fluid and natural it will become. You'll grow more self-aware and be able to quickly identify when and how to detach, thus making better decisions.

Equally important as being able to detach before prioritizing and executing is not becoming fixated on a single problem for too long. Part of honing this skill involves recognizing when the priority shifts, and you must change tactics. That's why prioritizing and executing is an ongoing strategy that helps you continually evaluate and reevaluate where your focus, energy, and resources need to be applied.

The benefit of this approach is that it trains you to stay a step or two ahead of your real-life problems. You develop contingency plans and become better equipped to anticipate challenges. That gives you time to strategize a response *before* a problem occurs. That's a major advantage that can keep you from becoming overwhelmed. Much like with first principles, prioritize and execute gives us the ability to gain valuable insights and new perspectives. And when we step back and see things from a different perspective, it opens up a whole new world of possibilities.

Complications naturally occur, and problems in one area can easily overflow into another, so it's important to consider this technique. For example, a relationship or health problem might take priority over your fusioneering vision. If you experience a financial complication, you might need to prioritize that before continuing this journey. If you don't address your top priorities, no matter what they are, it can negatively impact everything you do down the road.

This approach isn't new for me. I was doing a version of P&E long before I read about it in *Extreme Ownership*. Back when I started working at HP in 1978, I had to participate in a time-management class. They taught us how to be productive and efficient with our daily work and also how to think in terms of weekly, monthly, yearly, and five-year goals. HP used a process called Management by Objectives, whereas the people above would give me specific tasks to accomplish. In turn, I would pass along work objectives to those below me. I needed to be highly structured, organized, and efficient, because I was working with many different departments, including R&D, manufacturing, sales, and tech support, while simultaneously coordinating with those above me, our divisions around the world, and reporting back to HP corporate. These tools helped me become successful.

When I started building the robot years later, I wasn't assigning tasks to anyone. My life went from a complicated one to being simple and linear. I was a hermit working in my hobbit hole, following my energy, and doing whatever work interested me at the time. I drifted away from this structure because I didn't need it. Now, my life has gotten complicated again as I'm working on this book, along with four other projects, including a documentary video that will parallel and complement the sections of this book and a virtual reality tour of my studio, robot, and art galleries. I am juggling more balls, which requires me to be organized and efficient, so I've naturally reverted back to these techniques.

Without fail, every day, I do early morning P&E with a cup of coffee as I watch the sunrise. It's how I structure my day, and it's helped enormously. I jot down everything I need to do for the day and number those tasks according to priority. I also do this with my short-term and longer-term goals. I'm always clear about what I need to get done, and while I may be juggling many different balls, I always make sure that my top priority is being addressed. And I still use my leather Day-Timer from HP (which I got back in 1978) and do most of my work on yellow tablets. I'm a paper guy.

Whenever I go into a coffee shop to do some work, everyone else will have their laptops open, and I'll be there with my paper and pen. That process works for me. I'm visual, and I like seeing things laid out in front of me. It helps me prioritize and mentally work through problems and formulate new plans for moving forward.

Objectivity and the ability to look at problems from a different perspective are key components of both first-principle thinking and prioritizing and executing. However, you still need to solve the problem and be productive. That requires critical thinking and creativity. There is no better way to do that than by entering the state of flow!

How to Get into Flow

I realized early on that creativity and being more effectively creative would be essential for me as I moved forward. So I set out to learn as much as possible. I had a foot-tall stack of books on the subject of creativity, but far and away the most useful and well-researched book is *Creativity* by Mihaly Csikszentmihalyi.

Csikszentmihalyi's team interviewed highly successful creative people from all walks of life to learn what made their lives and work meaningful while trying to determine what made them so creative. The team talked to and studied an impressive group of artists, scientists (including many Nobel laureates), businesspeople, and statesmen who were at the top of their fields. They learned that the idea of the tormented artist didn't ring true, and life's struggle wasn't what made people creative. If anything, the opposite was true. Most lived normal, happy lives. However, he did discover one common denominator regarding their success. Their productivity didn't occur when they relaxed or escaped. It occurred when they were totally focused, immersed in their work, challenging themselves, pushing their limits, and oblivious to the outside world. Csikszentmihalyi referred to this state of mind as *flow*.

Flow is best described as the sensation of being so immersed in a task or activity and having such intense concentration that time flies by. You become oblivious to everything else. You have the potential to experience flow during any activity, from playing video games to washing the dishes. Even though it may sound like an escape, it's actually the opposite, because you become incredibly engaged.

When I first read this book back in 1997, I made the following handwritten notes about Csikszentmihalyi's attributes of flow:

- You have clear goals every step of the way. When in flow, you will always know what needs to be done.
- There will be immediate feedback on your actions, so you always know how you're doing.
- There is a balance between challenges and skills, so you feel your ability is suited to overcome obstacles and take action when opportunities present themselves. You don't experience the extremes of boredom and anxiety.
- Action and awareness merge to create extreme focus, so you can use your skills to overcome challenges. This becomes possible with clear goals and consistent feedback.
- Distractions are eliminated, so you only become aware of what is relevant at the moment. This intense concentration can alleviate the fears and anxiety of everyday life.
- There is no fear of failure because you're too focused on the task and what needs to get done.
- Self-consciousness evaporates, because you will be too involved in what you're doing to let your ego get in the way.
- Your sense of time gets distorted.
- You become autotelic, so enjoyment comes from the process, not the end result.

Understanding these attributes has consistently made it easier for me to get into flow. This isn't a rare phenomenon. You have most likely experienced it at some point yourself when doing something you love, like playing an instrument or working in the garden. I've experienced flow when programming or working on a painting. Time can become distorted; I'll look up and be shocked to see that two hours have slipped by. The same thing would occur when I was skiing down the zipper line of a double-black-diamond mogul run in Vail on a beautiful sunny afternoon. But if I missed a turn, I would suddenly be out of flow. When you're in flow, you aren't aware you're in it. But as soon as you take a misstep or become aware of your situation and surroundings, you're no longer in flow.

One key to getting into flow is that what you're doing is neither too easy nor too difficult. Let's say I'm a novice tennis player competing against an advanced player; neither of us will get into flow in that case. I'll be in over my head and frustrated, while the other player will be bored and unchallenged. The flow channel exists where your skills match the level of challenge. The activity needs to be engaging enough so that you aren't bored and not so difficult that you feel overwhelmed and stressed. We don't choose the obstacles we face, so we are naturally out of flow when trying to solve difficult problems. In these cases, it's important to break the problem down into smaller, more manageable pieces (just like with first principles and prioritize and execute), because that will allow us to get into flow more easily.

What's beautiful about the fusioneering process is that, by the time you start, you've already done much of the work that can help you enter flow when pursuing your vision. While engaging in the actions from your Seven Stories and getting in touch with what lights you up inside, you have a clear goal as you pursue your passion. You understand your innate intelligences, learning styles, and how you think. You've studied your domains, achieved the necessary levels of proficiency in the essential skill sets, and are pursuing something you love without expecting external results. You've fallen in love with the process. That makes it much easier to focus on the types of tasks that will allow you to remain in flow, so you can make progress. You know what you have to do and can cultivate the ideal circumstances to do it. Still, that doesn't always make it easy.

First principles, P&E, and flow—I call these the Big Three. Each has been instrumental in my success. I've turned to them for decades, so they are now inherently intuitive parts of my life. If you can master these techniques, so they become second nature, it will give you a tremendous advantage that can help you overcome obstacles, arrive at innovative breakthroughs, and make great strides as you move along on your journey. These concepts are all connected and feed off each other. By prioritizing, you're clearing your slate of distractions, so you can slide into a state of flow and be creative while working toward a solution. While in flow, you might suddenly have that priceless insight, or experience the wonderful feeling of that *aha* moment when everything comes together. This is one of the most rewarding feelings you can experience—much more rewarding than the temporary pleasure or escape that comes from instant gratification. This is because it's connected to your *ikigai*, your reason for being. You're improving, solving problems, and progressing in your attempt to bring your fusioneering vision to life.

CHAPTER 9

Traits to Embody on Your Journey

We all have different strengths and talents. Tapping into yours will serve you well, but you don't want to rely on your talents alone. There are a series of universal traits and skills that, if they are cultivated and honed, can aid you on your journey, no matter how unique your vision. If you can learn how to take calculated risks, remain curious, stay true to your values, and find the opportunity in obstacles, you will set yourself up for future success.

Taking Calculated Risks

James Cameron wrote, produced, and directed the film *Avatar*. It was released in 2009 and has since become the highest-grossing movie ever, making over $2.9 billion at the box office. It was a passion project that was many decades in the making. However, for the filmmaker to bring his vision to life and make the movie he wanted to, he couldn't just dive right in. He had to wait until the conditions were right for him to start.

Cameron was a filmmaker known for always pushing the envelope regarding CGI and digital effects. *Aliens*, *The Abyss*, and *The Terminator* films were all technically difficult to make. It was in Cameron's blood to challenge himself, and as the owner of a visual effects company, he constantly tried to exceed the limit of what was possible. After directing Arnold Schwarzenegger and Jamie Lee Curtis in the action comedy *True Lies*, with his next film, he wanted to return to what he was most passionate about and make the most high-tech film ever produced. He knew exactly the movie he wanted to make. Ironically, it was about a low-tech subject and an allegory for how our high-tech civilization has caused us to lose touch with nature.

Growing up in rural Canada, Cameron loved the outdoors. He was always out in the woods and around animals. However, that wasn't his only interest. He also had a love of art and science fiction. Even at a young age, his artistic (and fusioneering) sensibilities were keen: He would create and draw alien creatures inspired by the real-life animals he studied. Supposedly, he drew a picture back in the 1970s of a blue creature resembling the Na'vi in *Avatar*. That concept had lived in Cameron's mind for most of his life. Inspired by pulp sci-fi novels he used to read on the long bus rides to school, like *John Carter of Mars* and adventure stories such as *The Man Who Would Be King*, he developed a familiar adventure story in an unfamiliar environment. In 1995, he finally put pen to paper and wrote an eighty-page film treatment for *Avatar*.

At the time, Cameron was already in preproduction on his next blockbuster, *Titanic*, so the idea was to begin preparation for *Avatar* during the production of *Titanic*. He hoped to use the same computer animation techniques Steven Spielberg used to produce *Jurassic Park*, which had been released in 1993. However, as his team worked with the technology, they realized there was a big difference between using computer animation to create the dinosaurs for *Jurassic Park* and bringing main characters to life who must speak and have an unlimited range of expression. The facial capture technology required to do that was a long way off. It wasn't possible to make the film as Cameron envisioned it. He wasn't ready to start, so instead of compromising his vision by trying to push through, he recognized the limitations and put the passion project he had been thinking about for decades on the shelf. He then shifted his focus back to *Titanic*.

When *Titanic* was released in 1997, it became the largest-grossing film of its time. Cameron then produced a series of documentaries about deep-sea exploration. In 2005, ten years after he finished the eighty-page treatment, he turned his attention back to *Avatar*. While 3D technology had come a long way, the performance-capture technology essential to his vision still required development. However, he knew his domains and what the teams he worked with were capable of, so he was confident he could develop that technology. That's why he decided it was time to take a big risk, but a calculated one.

Knowing he wouldn't get a green light from Twentieth Century Fox to make *Avatar* right away, he made the studio an offer: Agree to fund the $10 million technological and conceptual development process that would determine the feasibility of the project, and if after seeing the pitch, they didn't like it, they could still pass. Knowing that the process would provide valuable insight into this technology for future films, Fox agreed.

Cameron and his team spent the better part of 2005 working on a film that they knew might not even get made. He oversaw two separate teams, each focusing on a crucial aspect of the process—technical and design. While the technical team researched the technology, the design team developed the art and visual look for the fictional world of Pandora. The goal was to create something that didn't resemble anything that had come before it. As the technology and design started to come together, Cameron turned his eighty-page treatment into a massive 200-plus-page script before eventually trimming it down to a more manageable 148-page draft. Having done their homework, Cameron and his teams made their pitch to Fox in January 2007. The studio was skeptical yet still green-lit the film. Now Cameron and his team had to go make the movie.

The story of James Cameron's lifelong journey to make *Avatar* is a master class in knowing when to wait and knowing when to take calculated risks. He didn't start too soon and wasn't afraid to put the project on hold. Ten years later, even though the technology wasn't exactly where it needed to be to make the movie he envisioned, he was confident his team could make it happen, so he took that calculated risk. It goes back to ensuring your heart and your head agree before deciding. It also critically involves knowing your domain, doing your homework, and setting realistic expectations so those calculated risks lead to major breakthroughs.

Always Remain Curious

During the five years spent working directly under Hector as a landscape architect, Tom learned the skills required to run the business. He studied other successful companies to better understand their keys to success. He visited job sites, viewed completed projects, and reached out to his clients to better understand their opinions and needs. The years spent working with Hector taught Tom the importance of building a quality team and managing people. His story is a textbook example of how a gradual start can lead to success.

When the date arrived for Hector's retirement, Tom paid him sixty percent up front to gain control of the company, becoming the majority owner. They had worked out a deal for Tom to buy the remainder of the company over the next ten years. As planned, Tom acquired a strong, viable business with fifteen employees, five active projects in various stages, and plenty of potential clients who could keep the company busy for years.

Because of how Tom utilized stepping-stone jobs, he had taken much of the risk out of his career change. He hadn't been earning as much money as he had at his previous job, and he did have to dig into a significant portion of his savings to make the initial payment to Hector. However, he and his wife had planned extremely well. They made sound investments and budgeted for all their expenses, including their children's tuition payments. Now that he was the owner of a successful business, he could start earning significantly more money than he had while at his previous job. The fact that he was working outside while engaging in visual work that lined up with his Seven Stories and innate intelligences while also being directly connected to his *ikigai* made the experience even more rewarding.

In the five years before Tom took over, he added tremendous value that helped to grow the company, so the business he inherited was much healthier and bigger than the business Hector was running when they first met. Tom didn't intend to do anything differently. He was just inherently curious and constantly asked questions. He didn't know what he didn't know, and by default, he also didn't know what he couldn't do or wasn't supposed to do. That can be an advantage in some cases. It can result in ideas that veterans with experience would never think of because they are counterintuitive to how things are "supposed to be done." That's exactly what happened with Tom.

Hector was good at what he did. He started from nothing, and over the previous thirty years, he had built a profitable and respected business. And he did most of it all by himself. While his business evolved and grew significantly over the decades, he did what felt comfortable and worked for him. He didn't make any major mistakes or have any regrets, but Tom, out of sheer curiosity, stumbled upon alternate ways of doing things.

Once Tom understood more about the business, his background

experience and knack for numbers helped the company save money when purchasing and leasing the necessary equipment. He even found a more cost-effective way to remove and dispose of dirt from their various job sites. When they found themselves purchasing and replanting many small trees, they decided to turn the back of Hector's vast property into a small tree farm. They would start with ten- to twelve-inch saplings and grow them to six- and seven-foot-tall trees that they would replant at the various job sites.

Tom may not have had experience working in this domain or profession, but what he did have was extensive experience in the corporate world. While not everything was applicable, he brought a new perspective to the table regarding accounting, budgeting, and managing the money the company earned.

Tom's takeover of the business was smooth but wasn't completely without problems. In the first few months, two employees left the company because they required better health coverage. Tom knew about the benefits package Hector provided his employees. He wasn't initially familiar with the ins and outs, but after learning more about the employees' problem and the specifics of the plan, he immediately understood why those employees needed to work for an employer with better health insurance. Still, it put him and the company in a bind.

Without panicking, Tom prioritized and executed. First, he made a deal with the two departing employees to finish the existing work for their current clients before leaving. Second, he met with his remaining employees to discuss their health coverage. He listened to their needs before doing his own research. Although he couldn't afford to enroll in the comprehensive plan that provided the type of high-end coverage his departing employees required, he did find a better plan that wouldn't cost the company extra money. He then turned his attention to replacing the two employees with experienced workers. He didn't want to hire just anyone to fill the roles, and good help was hard to find. Luckily, Tom had built up a healthy network of landscapers and laborers from his time working at the nursery. He was able to hire temporary help while he looked for the best qualified candidates to fill his full-time openings. And he left the door open for those temporary employees to become full-time if they proved to be a good fit.

Business slowed down for a little while, but Tom suffered no major financial losses. Had he not properly executed, he could have been left high and dry on his current jobs, risked other employees leaving, and not found the best possible people for the job. Instead, he put his employees first and was honest about everything going on with the business.

This story reflects how Tom acquired and grew the business, and overcame issues. Between all the lines, however, is his desire to understand all dimensions of the business, as first mentioned earlier, and this was driven by his innate curiosity.

Often, doing the right thing is best, but what happens when the right choice might cost you money and security? That's a much more difficult decision to make.

Don't Compromise Your Values

Having found an affordable apartment to rent in Helena, Sarah streamlined her belongings, packed up everything she could fit in her Jeep, and arranged for a moving company to deliver her furniture and large items shortly after her arrival. She didn't bring anything with her that she didn't absolutely need. What Sarah didn't have yet and couldn't get until she officially moved to the area and started her ranch accounting business was a paying client. This wasn't unexpected, and it was why she had made arrangements with her accounting firm in Seattle to continue working remotely once she moved.

Having worked as a big-time accountant for over a decade, Sarah understood the realities of the profession. She realized that to get clients of her own in Montana, she would need to lure them away from existing firms. She had previously met some of the accountants and administrative people at these firms during her upgrade. Many helped her better understand the business, so the idea of taking clients away from companies that had helped during her transition made her very uncomfortable. It put a damper on her experience. She knew there had to be a better way, so she revised her plan.

Sarah listed all the ranchers she'd met with who were receptive to working with a traveling accountant. Instead of trying to lure that client away from another firm, she contacted those firms to see if she could work for them as a traveling associate. She knew she could provide a service those clients were interested in. It wouldn't be the same as owning her own business, but she would be living her dream by traveling to ranches and practicing her trade.

It took a bit of legwork before Sarah found a small firm in Helena that was interested in what she had to offer. The firm had two clients they felt were better suited for Sarah's type of in-person service. The owner felt their relationship with those clients had deteriorated due to their inability to work together in person, so Sarah's proposition came at the perfect time. This arrangement could help the firm improve its relationship with these clients and demonstrate the appeal of these unique services to potential new clients. The firm had been looking to grow, and this would help them offer the same comprehensive service as the bigger firms. It was a win–win.

For the next three months, Sarah traveled back and forth between the two ranches, each two hours away from Helena. It wasn't long before she realized why the firm's owner found meeting with each client in person so difficult. And when tax season arrived, that was a road she found herself traveling much more frequently.

At first, Sarah enjoyed driving through the wide-open country. After a few round trips, though, the long drives started to take their toll. Sarah was exhausted. She was never at home. She spent a fortune on gas, and the backcountry dirt roads were hard on her aging Jeep. In rural Montana, she'd often have to drive out of her way just to reach a place to stay for the night before traveling home the next day. Worst of all, she was rarely outside and on the ranches among the animals. She wasn't living the vision she had imagined.

During her upgrade, Sarah had the idea to purchase a camper van, which could also serve as her mobile office, complete with computer, printer, filing cabinets, and solar cells on the roof to keep everything powered. She'd also need it to be a four-by-four with heavy suspension and rugged all-terrain tires, because ranches were often located at the end of a long, bumpy dirt road. This way, she wouldn't have to worry about making those long drives. She could come and go as she pleased. However, a camper van required a significant investment that she couldn't afford to make until her business was off the ground. Now that she was working with a firm, she realized she wouldn't have to pay for the van herself. She approached her boss, and they came to an arrangement that worked for both of them.

A year into her stay in Montana, Sarah was able to stop working part-time for her previous employer in Seattle. The camper van proved to be a tremendous success. She had grown close enough to the two main clients that they let her stay in the camper on their ranch when necessary. She wasn't doing nearly as much driving and enjoyed being on the ranches so much that she rarely opted to go home unless there wasn't any work for her to do. Meanwhile, word spread among the ranching community, and the firm added two more clients that Sarah would handle personally.

Sarah's story is another example of a gradual start that paid off. More important, she recognized her limitations and chose not to compromise her values by luring clients away from existing firms. That led to an arrangement better suited for her and her situation. She wasn't yet a business owner as she had envisioned. But she wasn't in any rush either because she was still doing what she loved. She realized that owning a business wasn't the part of her vision that mattered most to her; it was a means to an end. She knew she would get there eventually. In the meantime, she enjoyed the journey.

Finding Opportunities in Obstacles

Having found a cheap one-way flight and a deal on an inexpensive hotel room, Noah landed in Rio de Janeiro, ready to start fusing. He would stay at the hotel in Rio for a week before deciding whether to travel to a different location or stay longer.

It took a day for Noah to catch up on sleep and adapt to his new surroundings. He had prepared so well that he developed a new schedule once he settled in and was extremely productive. Still writing multiple articles a week for his clients back home, he set aside some time every morning to do that work while he was fresh. That left him the entire afternoon to explore the area and do the research needed for his actual travel writing. Having done his homework, he had a lengthy list of possible topics to write about, including tourist attractions, local food, festivals, historic sites, outdoor activities, local music, wildlife, nightlife, and local art.

After a week, Noah had started writing a handful of articles, but he wasn't happy with them. He couldn't say anything new or different from what other writers had said about the same topics. Meanwhile, he struggled to assimilate. Without a close group of friends to socialize with or any television in his hotel room, he got into the habit of writing at night. These weren't articles or samples he intended for anyone to read; he found comfort in writing about his experience for himself. After a week, he had to decide if he wanted to move on. Instead of traveling to a new city and starting over from scratch, he decided to keep working in Rio.

Noah found an inexpensive Airbnb in a part of the city he liked and booked it for the next two weeks. During that time, he was committed to improving his travel writing samples and brainstormed more original topics to help his articles stand out. However, one obstacle became obvious once he arrived in Brazil, and it continued to create new problems: the language barrier.

Having taken four years of high school Spanish and two years in college (a requirement for his English degree), Noah could speak conversational Spanish. However, they didn't speak Spanish in Brazil; they spoke Portuguese. Of course, Noah knew that going in but significantly underestimated how few people spoke English and how little Spanish resembled Portuguese. Luckily, enough people spoke English that he could get by. Still, he felt like an outsider and distant from the culture he hoped to assimilate into.

The straw that broke the camel's back occurred when he tried to travel off the beaten path and accidentally boarded the wrong bus. By the time he realized his mistake, the sun had gone down, and his cell phone had no service. Nobody on the bus spoke English, so he got off at the next stop and found himself in a bad neighborhood right when it started to rain. After an hour spent wandering around, he found a taxi stand and was lucky that one of the drivers spoke English. He explained his predicament and got a ride back to the Airbnb. He made it home safely. It was a nerve-racking evening that could have gone horribly wrong. However, there was a bigger problem on his mind.

Noah felt like a tourist, and as a tourist, he couldn't gain the perspective required to write the type of articles he wanted to write. That's why he was so unhappy with the work he'd produced so far. When he made that connection, he knew that he needed to learn Portuguese to bring his vision to life.

Noah had saved enough and still had money coming in, so he could afford to be flexible. That required slowing down his current article production to add another leg to his stool. Learning Portuguese became priority number one, so he dove in headfirst. He started with some online services and YouTube videos, but the approach didn't resonate, and he wasn't learning much. After a little research, he found an adult school nearby where he could start taking classes immediately. The expense was well worth it.

Classes met three times a week. There were twenty other students, including a few Americans. Most were from Central America. He learned quickly. More important, the class was fun, and he became friends with some of the other students.

The more time Noah spent in Brazil, the more his articles took on a fresh new slant. He was no longer writing about the typical tourist topics. He found himself writing the type of articles that would have been helpful for him to have read before he arrived. When he checked his email early one morning, he finally got the positive response he had been waiting weeks to hear.

"How to Live Like a Local in Rio without Knowing the Language" was the name of the article that captured the attention of the editor of a small travel blog. Noah had found a way to use his problem to open a door. The editor told him the type of articles she was looking for, and soon he was writing three articles a week for that blog. He wrote about the Rio he experienced, which gave his material a personal slant. He advised which neighborhoods were the best for outsiders and which ones to avoid. He wrote about the typical mistakes tourists make and turned his articles into useful guides for young people looking to travel on a budget.

After a few weeks of consistently writing articles for the travel blog, Noah reached out to his editor. He asked her for advice about how to help his work stand out. She gave him some tips and even agreed to introduce him to other editors in her network who might be interested in his work. She encouraged him to increase his social media presence, create a website, and try to cultivate an audience. It was all good advice that he took to heart and was committed to doing. However, one thing she said at the end of their conversation struck a chord. She briefly mentioned how some bigger publications might be interested in long-form articles.

Noah spent the next few days in his room, poring over the weeks' worth of journal entries he'd written at night to turn them into a five-thousand-word article that he could submit to print publications. It became a passion project, and after a week, he had written a solid article about his early struggles in Rio. He sent out queries and submitted the article to a handful of publications without expecting to hear anything back. He forgot all about it and returned to his travel writing. Then out of the blue, he received an email informing him that his article would be published in *The Atlantic*. He would earn a significant sum of money—much more than he had ever earned for his shorter articles.

That article was the break Noah needed to jump-start his career as a travel writer. He had taken his editor's advice about expanding his social media presence. Slowly, he began to develop a following so that by the time his long-form article was published, it significantly increased his profile and the size of his platform. Editors contacted him, and he was offered more writing opportunities for more money. With job security, Noah got to work planning his next trip, a tour of the Amazonian rainforest. By earning money writing while traveling through the part of the world that had fascinated him since childhood, Noah was living his dream.

Curiosity will help you push boundaries. Knowledge of your domain will prove invaluable when solving problems and calculating risks. These, along with staying true to your values and relying upon your strengths, will help bring your vision to life.

Given that, there is no replacement for dogged perseverance, a quality that pays dividends over time. Not everything will go according to plan, and that's okay. It's important to not get discouraged. Stay the course, and remain true to your values. I have personally overcome so many obstacles on my journey that I've developed confidence in my ability to work through the next problem and find a path forward. I don't know how long it will take or how difficult it will be, but I just shrug and am quietly confident I can do it.

CHAPTER 10

Startup Adjustments

One important lesson I've learned on my journey is that sometimes it is necessary to add an additional leg to your stool and loop back to upgrade. This is a natural part of the fusioneering process, as Noah experienced when he realized that he needed to learn Portuguese.

It was the year 2000 when the robot and I were ready to combine art and science to create our first painting together. I had made a rule for myself that I would never copy a photo, so what could we paint? At the time, I was curious about an AI technique called generative systems. It looked promising, so I wrote a generative AI program and experimented with it. The first painting was a simple landscape with flowers in the desert. The second was a geometric painting. While they were modest compositions compared to the work I do now, it was as exciting to create those first two paintings as it has been for any since.

Dulcinea's first painting. Year: 2001

Reflecting back, it was such an exhilarating time! My robot was working! I wanted to run it some more, create new paintings, and see what we could do together, but there was a glitch.

When taking art classes or working on an oil painting at my easel, I never thought much about changing paint colors. They were all nicely arranged around my palette directly in front of me. I didn't worry about washing my brush until I was done. So while building my robot, I assumed that I'd manually change jars of paint and wash the brush as needed. I even added a little electronic beeper circuit inside the robot's control cabinet to alert me when either was necessary. The computer screen would then indicate which color to load next or if it was time to wash the brush.

I realized constantly being on call was not how I wanted to spend

Dulcinea's second painting. Year: 2001

my time. That's when I decided to make my robot fully automated. Using first principles, I analyzed what features and capabilities I needed to add. The robot needed to exchange jars of paint, wash the brush as needed, and seal the paint after each use to prevent it from drying out. I also needed an accessible shelving system to hold the many paint jars. I didn't know how to do any of that, so I had to figure it out.

Paint Exchange

For the robot to exchange jars of paint, it needed an arm to pivot, extend, and grip, plus a way to access the many jars of paint colors that could be stored on accessible shelving. I quickly realized

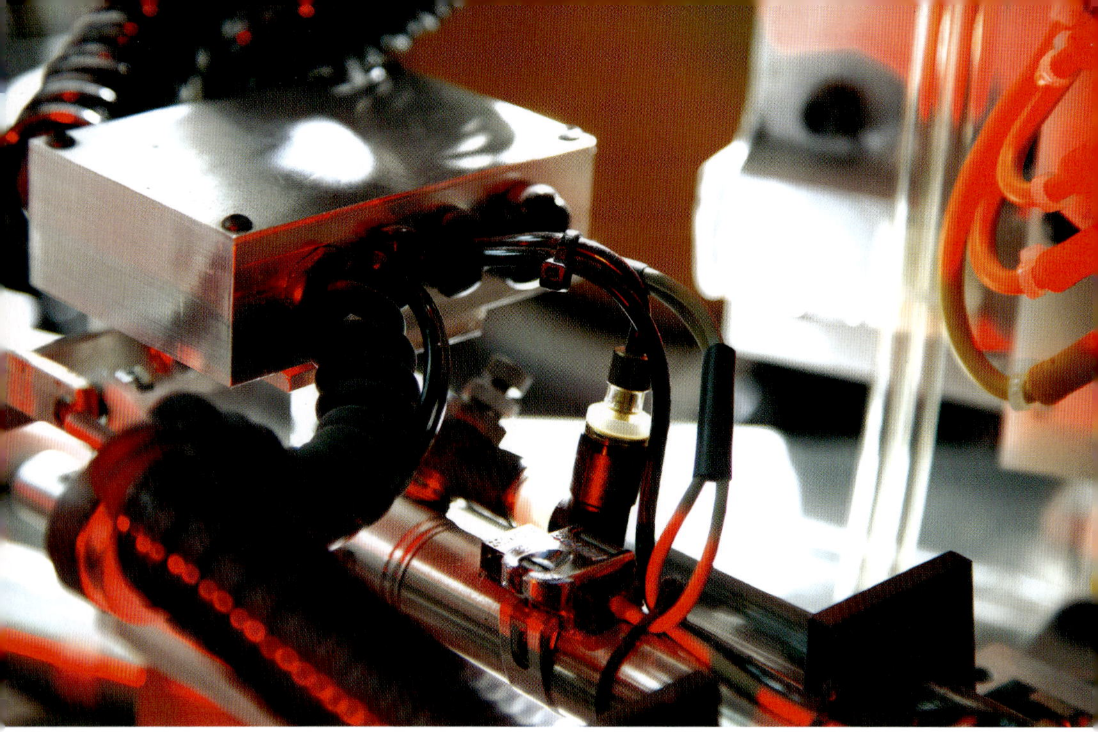

Close-up pneumatics for paint exchange

pneumatics could address the first part, and the robot's actual carriage system (that moves left, right, up, and down) could be used to index locations of paint jars on shelves for the pneumatic arm.

I mounted a pneumatic arm on the carriage under the robot's wrist and built shelves parallel to the carriage system that would hold the jars of paint. Through a location indexing system, the robot's carriage would move in front of a jar's location, then the arm would pivot to the jar, extend, grip the paint, retract and pivot back to the canvas, and extend once again to locate the paint under the robot's wrist. Once the system was built, it was fun to sit back and watch it operate as I had envisioned. Visitors also marvel as they watch.

Brush Washer

If the robot is going to change its own paint, it often needs to clean the brush before dipping it into a new jar of paint. How does it do that?

A fusioneer's playground: Dulcinea's wrist system, pneumatics, controls, and paint exchange

First, I had to install copper pipes for clean and dirty water from the utility room across the ceiling of the studio to the back of my steel structure, and then tubing routed on cable carriers on the robot's carriage to reach the wrist and brush. In the back was also a pump to return the dirty water during the washing process.

I built a plastic cylinder the size of a rounded half-gallon carton of milk. It would work like a vertical car wash, with twenty jets of water pointing down into the center of the cylinder. The robot would then move the brush up and down through this shower of water. I was ecstatic to see it all work for the first time, but my excitement was short-lived. When painting for an extended period, paint works its way deep into the bristles of a brush. When I learned the washer couldn't clean the brush properly, I cried for two days before figuring out what to try next.

The solution was to mimic what I would do as an artist when washing a brush full of acrylic paint: squish the brush up and down on the bottom of my industrial sink to spread out those bristles. So I created a plastic stool with a corrugated washboard for its seat inside the vertical washer. I'd run the water to flood the canister to an inch above the stool height. The robot would then squish the brush up, down, left, right, and twist it on the washboard to remove all of the paint.

This was a start. It worked well and cleaned all sizes of brushes. However, after the wash, a new problem arose. The robot's first brush was small, and it could get rid of the excess water in the bristles by pulling them up against the side of the brush washer's round opening in the top. With larger brushes, there was still too much water in the bristles, so the next strokes caused water and paint to run down the canvas.

Now what could I do to get that excess water out of the brushes? For medium-size brushes, I added a V-shaped notch in the round opening at the top of the washer. The robot could draw the bristles up through this notch to remove the excess water and then reshape them by pulling up again along the round opening at the top. That worked well. When I migrated to even larger brushes, it still wasn't enough, so I added a blow-drying system with my compressed air supply. It worked wonders, but a fine balance needed to be struck. The bristles couldn't be so dry that they couldn't be reshaped after the blow dry. All is well now, and it's a relief to have these automation features.

Not every color change requires washing the brush. However, in the instance of switching from a dark color to a lighter color or a completely different color, you might need to wash the brush before using the new color. It's also periodically necessary to wash the brush when using acrylic paints. Over time, the bristles will dry out and become stiff. To solve this problem, I added a software timer, set for twenty-five minutes, that triggers an automatic brush-washing sequence. Once the brush is washed, the timer is reset. The entire brush-washing process doesn't take much longer than a couple of minutes and uses about the same amount of water that is used when brushing your teeth.

Paint Sealer

Acrylic paint dries quickly, so the jars can't be uncovered for long. After struggling with this problem for a while, I'm proud of the eventual solution I devised to seal the jars. While I love sharing what I do in the hope that it can inspire others and help them learn, I do have one trade secret I don't want to share at this time. The eventual solution took some time to figure out and eventually combined multiple disciplines, and like Occam's Razor, it was straightforward to design and build.

The Third Painting

The year was 2003. My third painting was an ambitious one. I wrote the code for three types of AI (genetic programming, a form of artificial life; a rule-based expert system; and fuzzy logic) and was anxious to see the result. Since it required 3,500 brushstrokes, the robot needed to continue running overnight. At the end of the painting, after the last brushstroke, I programmed the computer to return the final jar of paint it was using to its location on the shelf of paints, seal it, wash the brush one last time, and park the carriage system in the lower-left corner of the structure.

That next morning, I was extremely nervous. *Did the program work and successfully run throughout the night and complete the painting?* As I unlocked the front door of the studio, I cautiously took two steps inside and looked sideways over to the robot. I breathed a sigh of relief when I saw that it had made its way back to the home position. I then mentally prepared myself to view the painting for the first time. Those first impressions are so valuable and cannot be duplicated. I was amazed and engrossed in viewing this new painting. I had done it! The robot successfully completed a painting, unattended and overnight. Suddenly, I realized something else, and I'll remember this moment forever. The

A true milestone: first fully automated painting, and painted overnight. 24" × 42". Brushstrokes: 3,500. Year: 2003

robot had turned its own power off! I was so absorbed in the painting that I hadn't noticed it at first. It now felt as if the robot was self-aware.

Earlier, I had added a simple bit of code as an afterthought only to forget all about it. Seeing that it had shut itself off was such an unanticipated and astonishing surprise. That's when another realization hit me. This 24-by-42-inch painting with 3,500 brushstrokes was probably the first in the history of man that was original artwork, created by an AI-based, fully automated robot. Not to mention it was painted unattended overnight.

This full automation process took a year to design and build. That was an amazing year, filled with creativity, learning, building, and problem solving. I still can't believe how much I accomplished in that time frame. That effort was what made the process so rewarding. I can't understate how empowering and gratifying it felt to conceptualize something, build it, and then sit back and watch it come to life.

It's only natural that you'll discover issues and problems along your Start phase, and you will have to work through them. Remember, you're working within your chosen domains, so think of them as offering growth opportunities, as these did for me.

Dulcinea Is Born

After nine years spent upgrading my skills and building my robot, we brought my vision to life and began our journey creating many paintings together. Now, having arrived at this moment, I felt it was time to give the robot a name. It couldn't be just any name. It had to fit the type of work we did together, and I eventually found the perfect one.

In *Don Quixote*, the hero aspires to be a knight and earn the love of a fair princess. Dulcinea is a hard-working peasant woman from a neighboring village who turns his head. Even though she never appears in the book and is only spoken of, it's clear that she makes an impression. That was the name I wanted to give the robot. Dulcinea. She works hard, never complains, and in my eyes, is a fair maiden.

Now that the robot had a name, I felt the paintings we completed together should have a signature. But who would sign it? Well, who painted it? She did. That meant it would be her signature. I created a program so Dulcinea could sign each painting. Developing the signature required a lot of iteration. It's amazing how your eye reacts to the small spacing between letters and the minute curves in a single scripted letter. Even a fraction of a millimeter affects how the letters in the signature are perceived. When crafting the signature, I added slight variations in the lettering, so it wouldn't look mechanical. It required subtle brushstrokes, pressure, and gestures, and now happily appears in all her paintings.

Dulcinea's signature mounted on the *z*-axis servo motor

The Process

While the art and the technology that inspires a painting concept can derive from an infinite number of sources, once I start a new painting, the development process usually involves the following stages. This might not exactly replicate the process you'll use in your own fusioneering journey, but it's a good place to start.

Concept

First, I start with concept: What is the idea behind the painting? What's its inspiration? What's the appeal for me? Before I commit to a new painting idea, it must satisfy four essential criteria:

- Does it excite me?
- Does the inherent challenge excite me?
- Will the painting captivate the viewer and entertain the eye?
- Will the painting create visual movement?

If any of these criteria are not met, I work the problem some more or move on.

Next, I'll try to evolve, define, and distill that original idea down into a single concise statement of concept. That clearly stated concept is the vision that will serve as my guide during the design and development of the painting.

Design

Once I've clearly and concisely defined my concept, I must next consider how to design it and technically create that art on the computer. Sometimes, even with the concept in hand, you have no idea how to create it. The artistic, creative struggle begins, but because this is your fusioneering domain, your unique vision and reason for being, you crave that challenge.

One possible idea occurred during a trip to Los Angeles for a wedding. While in town, my wife, Linda, and I stopped at the Getty Museum. In the Impressionist room, I saw one of Monet's paintings of the haystacks. I was so enamored with the glistening snow in the foreground that I went back into the room to view that painting two more times before we left. That's when I knew it would be a fascinating challenge to create an Impressionist-style painting using layers of color and brushwork similar to Monet's. I wanted to see Dulcinea make all those beautiful, small, dabbing brushstrokes of color. The artistic idea (or a glimmer of an idea) struck me first. That was quickly followed by the technical question of how to create that in the computer and turn it into brushstroke data for Dulcinea to paint. As usual, I had no idea how to do that. I had to get into the flow state and pursue many theories (and refer to first principles along the way) before eventually discovering a solution.

You'll recall that one of the very first rules I adopted for myself was to never, ever, copy a photograph. I don't believe copying is creative. While studying art and during my nine trips to Europe with Glenn Vilppu to study the masters, I determined that this rule was immutable. All my work must be original, so once I have my concept, I must figure out how to create the structure of the painting inside the computer using many layers of high-level coding. This process can go on for weeks or months, and that's perfectly okay because I love all the intense creativity involved. I'm living my fusion dream. Once the coding has evolved to the point that I really like what I see on the computer screen, I pass it along to the robot to paint it using hundreds (or thousands) of brushstrokes.

Impressionist. **48" × 54". Brushstrokes: 44,943. Year: 2005**

Once again lost in the precious *flow* space

Applying the Concept

While I've been talking about a painting, as you pursue your fusioneering dream, these same ideas may prove to be invaluable. You'll find, as I have, that when faced with a question, you'll often find the answer by referring back to your clearly and concisely defined concept. It will assist you in decision making and keep you heading in your intended direction, especially if you're getting sidetracked.

When painting a landscape, portrait, or still life, the colors needed for the painting are right in front of you. But when creating abstract art, what color scheme do you use? Where do you even start? You might initially ask what color scheme best captures that distilled concept for this painting.

There are so many possibilities and color schemes I could use for any given painting. Even small color shifts can significantly

GOLDEN
GOLDEN
GOLDEN
GOLDEN
GOLDEN
GOLDEN

Paul in his paint room, searching for answers

impact the mood, tone, and emotion of a painting, so finding the right colors requires a lot of work. That's why I have an entire room in my studio dedicated to storing paints and a giant work table for mixing colors to find just the right combination for the different elements of each painting. However, mixing paint colors the size of a quarter on my palette at the easel in front of me is one thing, but mixing pint-size jars of paint to the hue, chroma, and value I want is a completely different task. You have to keep adding, mixing, and stirring, testing, and then fine-tuning the color even more. It's much more difficult to get the colors right at scale.

The background color is also extremely important. It can have a dramatic impact, especially on the perceived visual depth of a painting. I have no way of knowing what I like and what works until I experiment with those combinations. I might also use plastic transparencies to see how certain colors look on top of other colors. Using a palette knife, I'll experiment by manually mixing color combinations onto heavyweight white paper. Oil paint is the same color when wet or dry. However, when acrylic paint dries, the color is noticeably darker, which can further complicate the color mixing process.

Colors can also look one way when mixing and then lend a different impression once on a large canvas. The applied paint thickness and the density of brushstrokes next to each other also affect the visual impression.

Once I develop my color scheme, mix the paints, and load them into their respective jars, the work is not yet done, because these colors might still need additional tuning during the next step.

In all this work developing the color scheme and mixing the palette of colors, when in doubt about which way to mix them or which way to go, the answer will most often be found by merely asking, "What was my distilled, driving concept?" With that in mind, you can make adjustments accordingly.

Developing the Gesture

Remember the watercolor I did of a castle on a neighboring hill, and how Glenn said I failed to capture the gesture? You'll recall that whenever you are creating an image, you're trying to capture the very essence of the scene. Without this, no matter how well implemented, your results will be lacking.

In general, the gesture means capturing the very essence of your image, that is, of whatever it is you're trying to achieve. For me and Dulcinea, the gesture might be considered at two levels. Is the painting working? Have I captured my distilled concept, the upward thrust of the towering castle on the adjacent mountain?

Then at the next level, I have the brushstroke—the heart and soul of painting! Why was there so much time and expense spent studying and building the wrist and then writing robotic code to execute those exquisite brushstrokes? It's all derived—at both levels—from the concept of my fusioneering vision, to fuse art and science, making paintings to behold, while implementing exquisite brushwork, just as the masters I studied. Thus you see the power of referring back to your initial concept.

For each brushstroke, I conceptualize the coding into what I call a "note," which contains a bundled set of information. For Dulcinea to complete a single brushstroke, she needs to know which brush to use; which color to use; how far to dip the brush's bristles into the paint; the number of strokes per dip of the paint; the angle of the brush throughout the stroke; the amount of brush rotation; the amount of pressure of the brush along the stroke; the speed, gesture, and style of each stroke; and the series of coordinates on the canvas along the stroke's length. Seeing the actual brushwork and paint on the canvas usually requires additional fine-tuning of the colors and brushwork, which is why I constantly loop back to the previous step and iterate. It can take months to get the colors just right, along with refining the brushwork.

Dulcinea capturing the essence of an awe-inspiring brushstroke

When working on any new painting, brushwork and color are the product of intense iterative development. Look at the brushwork in a van Gogh or Monet painting. Without their individual signature brushwork, what would you have? You quickly realize the significant role brushwork plays. Brushwork is so essential yet so often overlooked and taken for granted.

Iteration

That distilled vision I start with is my guiding force, so I naturally accept the challenge to produce something that captures and satisfies that vision. I may go through dozens of developmental canvases for a single painting. Your efforts may need iterations too. That's all good, since you'll be learning along the way, and eventually converging on your goal. We can imagine the iterations Noah, Tom, and Sarah experienced. Now's also the time, when working through these iterations, that being in *flow* might prove to be invaluable. When I'm mixing colors of paint into jars for a tentative palette and painting, I might be lost for hours.

Now for an iterative test run. For a small section of the painting, I'll load the jars of paint onto their respective shelf locations, secure some test canvas to the robot wall, and hit the run button. After Dulcinea makes fifty to one hundred brushstrokes, I have enough information to make the necessary large and small adjustments—texture, colors, background color, brushwork, and so on—and then iterate. Although perhaps painstaking at times, I've embraced the process, since I know that, with perseverance, I'll eventually reach my goal, that glimmer of concept, that initial glistening snow, leading to this painting.

After perhaps several versions of this, I'll conduct a test run for the entire painting. If it's more than a few hundred brushstrokes, I'll just let it run overnight and come back to view it in the morning.

Whenever I enter the studio in the morning after Dulcinea has created a painting overnight, I don't view it right away. I purposefully avoid it. I'll put my lunch in the refrigerator and make a cup of coffee before setting up my director's chair and TV tray (arranged with yellow notepads) in front of the painting. Then I'll view it for the first time and get that invaluable first impression. I look for the overall feeling and ask myself if the painting works as I intended.

This is a valuable moment. With patience, many things will appear that I want to improve upon, whether it be brushwork, the colors, or the overall design. Sometimes I'm just stumped and don't know how to proceed.

Each of these areas has a major impact upon the painting. So I repeat this iterative process until I have a canvas I'm happy with. I then mount the full-size canvas on my big easel and look at it from a distance across the studio. Monet said you have to walk a mile to develop one painting, which means you have to step back from the painting and view it at a distance. The process now begins anew with a new round of notes and items to tweak.

I have a "no shrugging" rule, which means that the work can't be just close enough or just okay. It must fulfill my original vision, and that doesn't often happen on the first try. I'm used to and gladly accept this iterative evolution; it's a crucial part of the process. The English art critic, painter, novelist, and poet John Berger summed it up best when he said, "Every successful work was the result of a long successful struggle. Innumerable works involved no struggle. There were also prolonged yet unsuccessful struggles." Don't avoid the struggle; embrace it. Your work will benefit from it.

I once read that a craftsman is focused on the thing he is making, whereas an artist is concerned if what he's working on is fulfilling his vision. For example, if you're a seamstress working on a film and must create a gown, that's the immediate task. However, on a higher level, you must ensure the design encapsulates the vision for that scene. As I move forward with each painting, I keep both perspectives in mind. Am I fulfilling my vision?

The secret to all this is to simply enjoy each day of the journey. I've also learned there is always room to evolve, and that's the next phase of this fusioneering process.

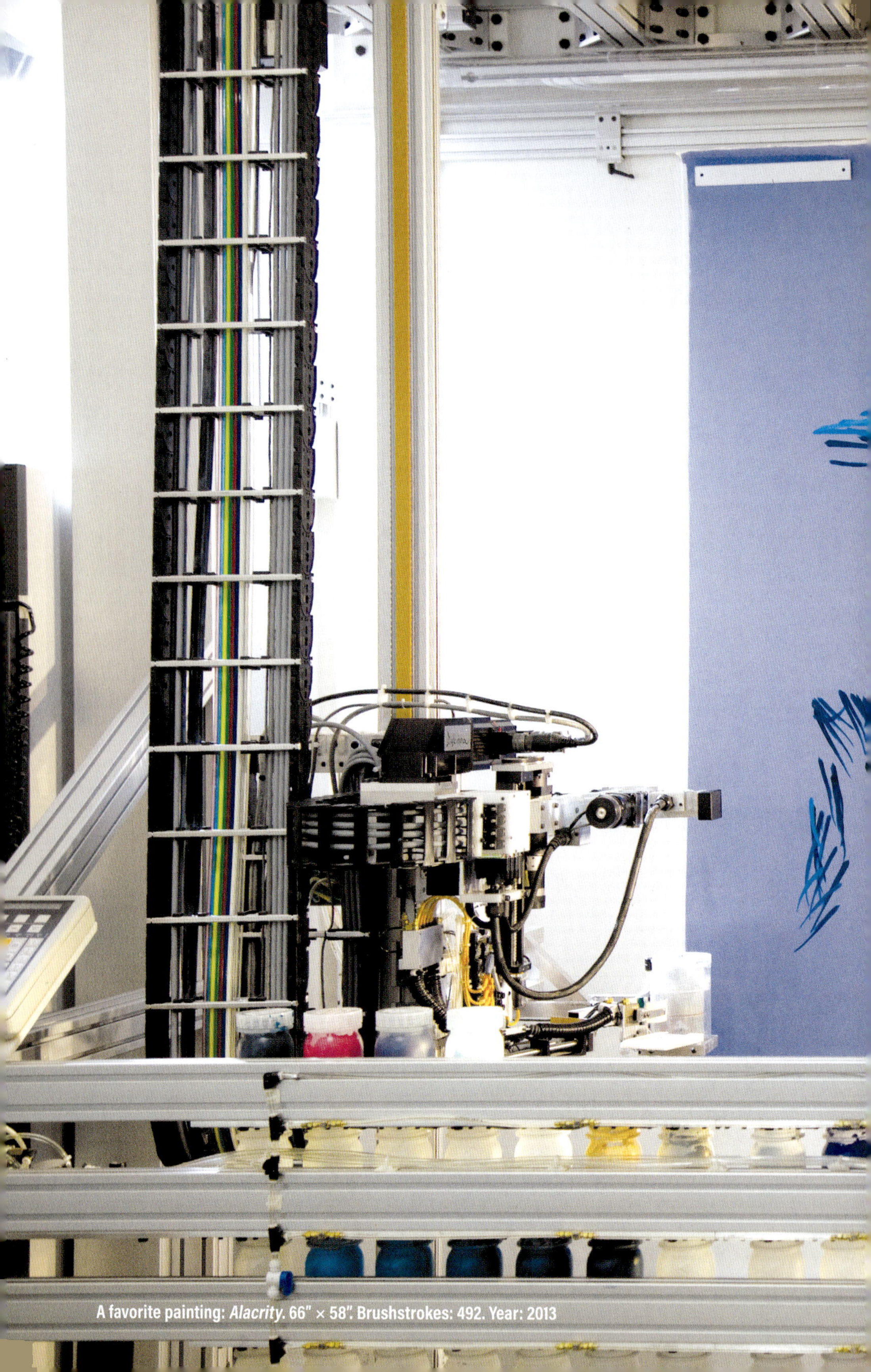

A favorite painting: *Alacrity*. 66" × 58". Brushstrokes: 492. Year: 2013

PART 4

EVOLVE

While the Start phase is about doing, building, and creating, the Evolve phase is about growing and progressing.

Your vision has been evolving since the beginning of your journey and will continue to evolve throughout this process. Every challenge you've overcome, every problem you've solved, is a form of evolution that can help you along your chosen path. However, the type of evolution that occurs during this phase is also a state of mind. It's about striving to grow, not being content doing the same thing over and over or taking the easy path. It requires earnest focus and dedicated work. You must challenge yourself to continually evolve your skills and work. Your ongoing growth and achievements will provide a natural sense of satisfaction and accomplishment. And since you're following your reason for being, you will experience pure joy and want to continue challenging yourself as you progress forward along your path.

The way you evolve can differ significantly depending on your circumstances, as can your need to evolve. It might be born out of necessity when you're forced to solve a problem. It might be a choice, such as expanding a business or taking on a new challenge.

No matter how you're evolving, this is the most rewarding part of the journey. While it may be the last phase of the process, it certainly isn't the end. In many ways, your journey is only beginning; this will become an ongoing way of life. That's the joy and beauty of fusioneering.

As with every step of the fusioneering process, there will be obstacles that you must work your way through. Self-doubts may arise, and those doubts can lead to more questions. While the problems you encounter may differ during this stage, the approach to solving them remains the same, and you already have the tools, specifically the Big Three (first principles, prioritize and execute, and flow) to work through your problems. Combine that with the knowledge and assurance that you've solved other difficult problems throughout your journey, and you'll have the confidence to remain on the path and trust the process. You will know that you can push through the messiness and tension to emerge on the other side having evolved.

What's so special about this phase is that, as a fusioneer, you are now in a position to break new ground by combining attributes from multiple domains to develop a unique fused solution. Because you have refined skill sets in multiple disciplines, you have distinctive insights and can come to conclusions that someone familiar with only one discipline might not. That makes a fusioneer better equipped to arrive at original and groundbreaking solutions when searching for answers. I've experienced this firsthand, as have some of the most accomplished fusioneers throughout history who have achieved what many believed impossible.

The Evolve phase is where some of your most significant, transformational, and rewarding breakthroughs occur. It's where you will expand your vision and achieve what you didn't dream possible when you started on this journey. What you can accomplish is limitless. The secret is to not lose sight of what got you this far and remain grounded. You'll want to embrace two crucial components that will help you evolve naturally: curiosity and creativity. When you're curious, you can't help but ask questions that lead you to new ideas. Those ideas are rarely fully formed. They simply hint at the possibilities. While curiosity is what opens the door, creativity is what allows you to walk through it. This is true whether you're working in a creative domain or not. You just have to tap into the creativity that already lives within you.

An unexpected and pleasant phenomenon will occur while your pathway unfolds and you strive forward. You'll find happiness and enjoyment all along the way, because you are doing what you were meant to be doing, living your dream and purpose. The destination is the compass heading, but the journey becomes the fulfilling reward.

As a fusioneer, you've evolved well beyond where you were when you started. In this Evolve phase, you'll truly experience the integrated power of fusing all your stool's legs supporting your vision. One or two legs might work, but creatively combining all these disciplines may lead to wondrous opportunities and fulfillment. Open yourself to possibilities you might never have imagined possible. In Evolve, pause for a moment, reflect, and now creatively reach for even newer heights.

CHAPTER 11

The Three Pillars of Creativity

Your vision will be the source of your energy and what gives you resolve. Curiosity is what sparks new ideas. Perseverance is what keeps you going. The proven ability to problem-solve and overcome obstacles gives you confidence and assurance that you will find a way forward. Creativity allows you to grow, break new ground, and evolve.

Early on, knowing that creativity would play a major role in what I was attempting, I read a stack of books on the subject. I'd throw almost all of them out. However, I'd keep *Creativity* and the work of Mihaly Csikszentmihalyi. Understanding his insights and the state of flow, with its inherent attributes, proved invaluable when it came to being more creative. Reading about Leonardo da Vinci and learning how he worked also shed light on creativity. So what can you do to become more creative? How do you lay the necessary groundwork? I've condensed everything I've read into three key pillars:

- Know Your Domain
- Collaborate
- Experiment

I've learned from my art teachers, David Leffel and Glenn Vilppu, and a robotics expert, Glenn Helmes, who briefly visited the studio to assist with robotic issues. Collaboration for me was a bit different from what you might imagine. Perhaps because of the nature of what I'm doing, I never experienced that back-and-forth collaborating discussion between two people. Instead, Dulcinea became my de facto collaborator. Together, we'd try out and test new concepts, coding algorithms, or components of a painting all along the way. What would this look like? Dulcinea might tell me, through the way she produces her work, "I think the coding for those new brushstrokes you just made needs more work" or "Are those colors you just painted working?" If the overall design is not evolving properly, I'll need to rethink and try a new approach.

Most important, while collaborating with Dulcinea, I've relied on intense experimentation and extensive study in my domains of art and science. I am always striving to learn more and constantly experimenting with new ideas for a painting, designs, colors, textures, and robotic brushwork. Those three essential pillars just come naturally to me now.

While there is no one right way to tap into your creativity, the most successful fusioneers find ways to apply these pillars in the daily pursuit of their vision.

Know Your Domain

After two years working for a small accounting firm, Sarah expanded her role and established herself as a specialty service provider who did all of her work in person and on-site. Word spread among the

One of Paul's favorite domains of study

ranchers, and Sarah helped her firm win ten new clients she personally serviced.

The way Sarah ran her side of the business was to dedicate specific blocks of time to each of her clients, typically between two and five days, when she would meet with them in person to address their various accounting needs. She'd often travel from ranch to ranch to ranch, so there were some stretches where she was away from home for long periods of time. She soon grew close to her clients, so they had no problem letting her stay in her camper on their property. They trusted her, and it stemmed from her deep knowledge and understanding of her domain. She saved them money and made it clear that she was looking out for *their* best interests, not the firm she worked for. They saw that she could have charged them extra and didn't. That's what made those ranchers clients for life. It didn't take long for her to become a part of their family.

It had been years since Sarah had ridden a horse. She had always loved animals, but when she became a busy professional back in Seattle, she didn't have the same opportunity to be around them. So when one of the ranch hands offered to take her riding, she jumped at the chance. This was an integral part of her vision. During that summer, she experienced the joy of riding again, especially in such a beautiful setting. While spending time at another ranch, she befriended a group of female ranch hands who took her fishing for the first time. Every time she returned to that ranch, that same group made time to fish together at the lake.

Sarah's life had completely transformed in the time since she'd left Seattle. However, she kept in touch with her former colleagues in Seattle and contacts at her alma mater, the University of Washington, so when one of the ranchers told her that his daughter was applying, Sarah wrote a recommendation for her. The ranching family couldn't have been more grateful. When they invited Sarah over to celebrate their daughter's acceptance to the school, the rancher talked about an old friend named Nick who owned a ranch in a remote part of Montana. Nick's operation was completely different from theirs. In addition to cattle, it included timber and mining businesses, which each required a special set of accounting skills. The rancher felt that Nick desperately needed a skilled accountant, because he was old school and still did everything himself, so he suggested that Sarah work with him. She knew nothing about the mining and timber businesses and told him that she wouldn't be a good fit.

Days after that dinner conversation, Sarah continued to think about Nick and his accounting situation. *Why couldn't she do it?* She hadn't known anything about ranch accounting and Montana law when she started her journey, and she had quickly upgraded her skills in those domains. She could do the same thing again. And if she did, it would evolve her accounting business by allowing her to work with new clients who had timber and mining businesses.

After finishing her current work at the ranch, Sarah had a week before she needed to call upon a different ranching client, so she returned to her apartment in Helena, where she began investigating this new facet of her vision. She read everything possible about these new domains. She even reached out to her former Seattle colleagues who had previous experience working in these areas. It only took a few days for her to feel comfortable and realize that not only was evolving her business feasible, but it had the potential to be extremely profitable, as well as personally rewarding.

Sarah put together a pitch, and before leaving town, she met with her boss to lay out her proposal for evolving the business. Her boss had the same negative knee-jerk reaction as Sarah's when she first heard the idea. After ten minutes, the boss was completely on board. They decided to move forward but take it slow. The first step was for her to meet with Nick on his remote ranch.

Nick gave Sarah a warm welcome upon her arrival. He then gave her a tour of his operations and the vast ranch, which was tens of thousands of acres. The ranch was beautiful and encompassed a rich variety of forested lands, meadows, rocky hills, and mountain formations. The overall operation was like nothing she had ever seen. Before her visit, she had spoken to some of her colleagues and people in her network familiar with mining and timber businesses. However, seeing it all in person brought the entire situation and the scope of the potential job into focus. She instantly knew that this evolution of her vision would certainly be challenging, but having worked through problems before, she was sure she could do it again.

That night, Nick and his wife hosted Sarah for dinner at the main ranch house. They spent the first twenty minutes speaking about business and the next three hours telling stories and getting to know each other. By the night's end, Nick made it clear that he hoped they could work together. They got along so well that the ranching family offered her access to the well-maintained guest house on the property when she worked on their ranch.

The next day, Sarah returned home and reported to the owner of the accounting firm about Nick's ranch and their firm's expansion into the mining and timber accounting businesses. In the two years since Sarah began working at the firm, they had expanded their client list, and Sarah was a major reason why. That hadn't gone unnoticed. As a result, the firm's owner offered Sarah a partnership.

Sarah had a knack for networking. It's what gave her a jump start on her journey and helped her get ahead when she started out. However, it was the knowledge of her domain that proved to be the secret to the evolution of her vision. Sarah had a strong foundation in accounting, but when she started her adventure in Montana, she wasn't well versed in the specific areas of ranch accounting that would become her focus. Through dedication and persistence, she upgraded her skill set and became a trusted expert. She was not only knowledgeable; she made the clients feel comfortable. That's what set her apart and allowed her to evolve the business. Sarah was responsible for most of her evolution alone, but nobody is forced to do it all by themselves.

Collaborate

Noah had been working steadily as a travel writer for eighteen months. He had traveled to nine of the twelve South American countries; only Venezuela, Bolivia, and Suriname remained on his list. And while he was able to get the occasional high-profile writing job, they were few and far between, and they didn't pay enough for him to stop writing for other sites and publications. Luckily, he maintained good relationships with all the editors he had written for, even the nontravel writing jobs, so he could work consistently and earn a steady income. However, it felt like he had reached the ceiling of what he could earn. He wasn't struggling, but he wasn't getting ahead either. It was as if his business and his fusioneering vision had plateaued.

Even though Noah had been traveling throughout South America for over a year, he managed to keep his expenses low. Through a new friend, he found a nice apartment in Rio that served as a home base. It was inexpensive, and the owner decreased the rent even more because Noah tutored his daughter in English. He had grown so used to saving money when working through college that it didn't feel like a sacrifice.

That mindset carried over to his professional life. Since he saved his money and the cost of living was low in Rio, Noah had been able to put some money aside. That gave him the financial freedom to accept unique writing assignments when they presented themselves, which is exactly what happened when he was asked to write an article for a prominent travel magazine about the history and architecture of French Guiana. This article would provide the largest fee he had ever earned (plus his expenses were paid) and would be featured in the most prominent magazine he had ever been published in. This would also be the first time he was assigned an accompanying photographer to work with. They were given a specific itinerary and a series of locations that required written and photographic content, so he and the photographer would need to collaborate. It was the opportunity of a lifetime and another job that could help define Noah's career.

Noah had to leave on short notice, six days after it was offered. Luckily, he had prepared to take advantage of these opportunities when they presented themselves, so he could pick up and go at a moment's notice. During those six days, he researched French Guiana and accepted more writing work to earn additional money. He wanted to enjoy the sites and experience the culture in French Guiana without worrying about other work or financial obligations. This was all a major part of his original vision to experience the region and its people, so it was important that he had time to enjoy the locations he visited and not fall into a trap where his work became just another job.

Once on the ground in French Guiana, Noah met Miguel, the photographer, at the airport. Together, they split a taxi ride to the hotel where they would stay for the weeklong assignment. During the first evening, they brainstormed ideas and got organized for their assignment. They had a lot in common and quickly became friends. Miguel was in his late twenties. He grew up in Mexico City and went to college in Los Angeles before becoming a digital nomad, making a name for himself as a photographer. He was on a journey similar to Noah's, so they experienced the same challenges. Most important, they shared the same interests. They loved traveling to different parts of the world and experiencing new cultures.

The work Noah and Miguel teamed up to create was the best either of them had ever done. They worked extremely well together, and each learned a little more about the other's craft. The article and the pictures were phenomenal. The editor was duly impressed. Before they went their separate ways, Miguel gave Noah one of his old cameras, so he could experiment with the photojournalism techniques he had learned on the trip. That planted a seed.

Once he was back in Rio, Noah resumed his other writing work. He also returned to the Upgrade phase to learn more about photojournalism and how to incorporate pictures into his articles. He reached out to the editors he worked with and the people in his network to get ideas for how he could evolve his business. This opened new doors and created new possibilities.

Given how difficult it had been for Noah to get his writing career off the ground when he began the Start phase, he anticipated the same type of resistance and struggle during Evolve. He assumed it would take him a long time to find sites and publications interested in articles accompanied by photos. However, the opposite was true. At this point, he had experience and hundreds of writing samples, including some in prominent publications, which made his work more appealing to potential editors. This changed the scope of his business. He started getting more work that allowed him to incorporate his photojournalism. These assignments paid well, and he soon earned enough money that he didn't have to write as many articles just to stay afloat. He finally felt a sense of relief.

After the article about French Guiana was published, it also raised his profile as a travel writer. Other publications he hadn't worked with before started contacting him about possible assignments. They didn't all involve photojournalism. He still wrote traditional articles without photos. However, the inclusion of photojournalism evolved his vision, transformed his business model, and allowed him to surpass the plateau that had left him feeling stuck.

Six months after returning from French Guiana, Noah was awarded another lucrative travel writing assignment. This one took him out of South America and required him to travel to the Croatian coast for a week to write about local food. There, he would be reunited with Miguel, whom he had remained in contact with over the past six months. Once again, they worked extremely well together and produced compelling, visually appealing work.

On their last night in Croatia, Noah and Miguel discussed possibly working together beyond their own assignment work. Miguel explained how, during the past six months, he had been working on and off with an American YouTuber named Nicole, who was based out of Paris and had developed a significant following as a travel vlogger. Miguel would shoot videos, and Nicole was the face in front of the camera. Miguel helped improve the quality of her videos, which led to more views and a spike in her popularity. That meant they earned significantly more money. However, it felt like their videos were getting stale and repetitive. They needed a fresh slant, so Miguel suggested that Noah come on board as a writer to help evolve their content.

Knowing nothing about video production nor how his writing skills would apply to YouTube videos, Noah was skeptical. However, Miguel convinced him to meet with Nicole the following week in Paris. Noah went into their meeting with an open mind but was doubtful he could contribute. He was wrong. Once they started discussing potential video concepts, Noah's ideas about which locations to visit, what topics to cover, and how to curate their content to give it an original slant proved immensely valuable. All of the skills he had acquired and sharpened while writing travel articles could be applied to this new domain of video production. He even surprised himself with how valuable his contribution could be to the overall process.

The trio decided to shoot a series of five short travel videos in Paris over the following week. Drawing on his previous experience with what travel content stood out as unique, Noah helped the group develop topic ideas and narratives. Even though he wasn't familiar with the area, he knew how to get around in a foreign country. He had a knack for communicating with the locals, who helped him find the city's hidden gems. There was a loose, impulsive, do-it-yourself style to how the trio worked together.

When they had enough material on video, Noah returned home to Rio, and the group stayed in touch as Nicole rolled out the five videos over the next three weeks. These videos received more views and likes than any of her previous content. The experiment worked well and was extremely lucrative. Noah made almost as much money assisting with those videos as he could have writing articles over a three-month period. The trio decided to unofficially go into business together and made plans to shoot another series of videos the following month in Barcelona.

Meanwhile, Noah continued his travel writing work, and because the YouTube projects were so lucrative, he could finally afford to be more selective in the writing work he accepted. He could write fewer articles while earning more money. That gave him more time to dedicate to each project.

In addition to evolving his business, Noah evolved as a fusioneer because he found a way to expand beyond the confines of just travel writing. His writing skills opened the door to new possibilities. Noah never considered photography, video, or YouTube as a viable outlet for his vision, yet that allowed him to take his travel writing skills to an entirely new level. Once he started collaborating with Miguel and Nicole, he was presented with a new world of opportunities. The videos accompanied by the prestige articles he wrote significantly increased his brand recognition and online profile, which increased the number of incoming calls he received for potential work.

Noah was responsible for his success and did most of his work completely alone, without any outside help. However, through collaboration with Miguel and Nicole, he was able to evolve. He used his skills, knowledge, and expertise to contribute to a group effort that produced something on a level that none of them could accomplish on their own. By working with them, he was able to add photojournalism and video skills to complement his writing skills. Now, by fusing them, he could offer ever more attractive services.

Noah's evolution wasn't the product of luck. Through dogged persistence, a belief in himself, and a desire to evolve, he created exciting, new opportunities for himself. Noah saw an opportunity, and he took it. However, you can't always wait for opportunities to fall into your lap. Finding a way to break new ground might require a willingness to venture forward on your own through experimentation.

Experiment

After ten years as the sole owner of a landscape architecture business, Tom had come an incredibly long way. His journey began with a part-time summer job in a local nursery, and he evolved to become a well-regarded landscape architect in northern Colorado. After taking over from Hector five years earlier, he'd tripled the size of the business. His family was financially comfortable. His employees were happy. There was more work than the business could handle. He could keep expanding if he wanted to, but Tom was experiencing a different problem: complacency.

While growing the business over the years, Tom had lost touch with what he fell in love with at the beginning of his journey. He enjoyed the outdoors and design, but somewhere along the way, his dream became work. It didn't excite him anymore. By this point, he had delegated most of his responsibilities and didn't have to deal with much of the day-to-day business. He knew it was a good problem to have, and after the challenges that came with changing careers, he wasn't complaining. That's why he'd let it go on for so long. He thought about it and finally spoke with his family and friends, but he didn't get any satisfactory answers or insights. He realized he wanted to get back to doing what excited him. He revisited his Seven Stories, reconsidered his intelligences, and explored his *ikigai*. This time, he did not have the money constraints he had before, so he had time to explore some new ideas.

Tom didn't get the answer he was looking for immediately. He spent time carefully reviewing what excited him, and that's when he recalled the joy he felt during that college architecture class he took years earlier. He revisited the work of the architects he studied, and as he read about them with a fresh set of eyes, he saw a common theme in the designs that spoke to him: water. It was fun to reminisce, and he thought of his days growing up fishing in the local streams, but he couldn't see how water would apply to his work and vision. He went to bed that night only to wake up at four in the morning after experiencing an epiphany: He could expand his business by adding the complementary landscaping service of installing ponds and attractive water features.

Tom never went back to sleep. He immediately started learning about the business and studying existing firms. He was clearly in the state of flow, because it was eleven o'clock before he realized it. This was a brand-new idea, and he didn't know if he could make it work, but he had not felt this level of excitement in a long time. It was a natural evolution of his original vision. He was fusioneering again, combining the things he loved with a renewed sense of vigor.

This time around, Tom was in a completely different situation. Because he had succeeded in growing the business, he had the freedom to experiment with ways to evolve and grow both himself and the business. He couldn't be reckless, because he had employees to support, and they relied on the business for a paycheck. He wasn't going to put their livelihood in jeopardy. He crunched the numbers to determine what money, time, and resources he could devote to a trial period for pursuing this idea. With that, Tom returned to the Upgrade phase and spent the next month learning everything possible about designing and building world-class ponds and water features. That included tiered water fountains and how they could attractively augment his current landscape design offerings.

Building ponds required an entirely new skill, a trained crew, and large, specialized equipment for excavation and transporting and installing heavy rocks and boulders. This would be a big jump for Tom. He knew he was taking a risk. This was a specialized product, and he didn't know the size of the market or whether it would be receptive to his services. However, the more he learned about the business and the competition, the more he perceived what was creatively possible, and that excited him.

Tom wanted to gain some pond-installation experience before undertaking a project for clients, but the lack of a track record made finding a paying client difficult. He did have his reputation as a landscaper, and after ten years in the business, he had many contacts in the construction field. He reached out to a contractor friend who was overseeing the building of high-end subdivision homes. They negotiated a deal for Tom and his crew to construct pond features for three of the homes. They were simple in design but would be augmented with his attractive, complementary landscaping. With his current business running smoothly, Tom now had some time and the freedom to learn the craft and experiment with different designs and techniques. He and his crew made some mistakes on that first job but learned from them and quickly recovered. Their finished work was eye-catching. His contractor friend was pleased, and in addition to gaining some references, he and his crew also gained valuable experience.

Tom and his company were subsequently awarded two new landscaping contracts that would also have pond features. He was excited because he could use his visionary architectural skill to have the installations beautifully designed. That first year, the pond business was naturally slow, and after having to acquire all the necessary equipment, the company had yet to turn a profit. However, Tom had prepared for that. He had set money aside, so he would have time to learn and grow the business without sacrificing the company's financial stability. Through it all, he didn't get discouraged and approached this new evolution just as he had his main vision: with dogged persistence, a reliance upon his new skill sets, and confidence from having worked through similar problems before. He learned from as many people as possible. He studied existing work and learned more about design. He got back to his architectural roots and reacquainted himself with the masters whose work he originally fell in love with. With that fusioneering excitement rekindled, he started drafting and exploring intriguing new landscaping ideas, including beautifully sculpted ponds and tumbling water features.

Meanwhile, the pond work gradually began to increase. With his love of architecture and his visual intelligence, he began to incorporate aesthetic design elements into his pond work. These weren't just circular ponds anymore. They had irregular designs, waterfalls, rock overhangs, goldfish tunnels, and solar-powered lights that automatically turned on at night. Since he was already a landscape architect, he could seamlessly and artistically incorporate these designs into the overall installation for each property.

This pond work renewed Tom's passion. He sought experts to help him create a website and build a social media presence to showcase his work. During his upgrade, he learned of a national competition for pond installations, which he hoped to enter one day. Pond people loved to talk about ponds, and he soon became part of a unique subculture of people who shared his passion. In the process, he learned from them and leveraged that knowledge into his business.

Two years after he started the pond business, it finally turned a profit, and he grew more comfortable with the business model. It turned out, pond owners also wanted expert advice on how to maintain clear water and control algae, and they needed annual pond cleanings. This enhanced his business and ensured it would only grow with time. Tom turned much of the management of the main landscape architecture business over to his senior employees, so he could focus on his new pond passion. After feeling complacent for a few years, this work made him feel alive again.

Tom's hard work had paid off, and he had the financial resources to continue experimenting with how to evolve his business. Armed with the confidence gained from surviving difficulties before, he trusted the process, as he had learned to do, and eventually, everything worked out.

Experimentation can differ for everyone, and how you experiment will depend on your objectives. No matter what your approach, experimentation is a powerful third pillar that will empower you to be more creative.

Together, these three pillars—knowing your domain, collaboration, and experimentation—will serve you well in your quest to be more creative while on your fusioneering journey. While they certainly aren't the only ways to become more creative, you'll find them to be most effective. By this stage in the process, you will have gained valuable experience and a much better sense of how to use the various tools at your disposal. You'll experience that creative thrill and sense of joy as you continually grow.

CHAPTER 12

The Joy of Always Striving Forward

The Evolve phase is a highly personalized phase and can mean different things to different fusioneers. How you choose to evolve can also differ significantly depending on your vision. I have been evolving for over twenty years; every new painting is a form of evolution. The artistic and technical concepts and methodologies for each painting have evolved and will continue to do so. As soon as one painting is completed, I immediately challenge myself to seek out exciting new ideas and concepts for the next one. I'm always striving, always evolving.

When searching for a new artistic concept, I can be inspired by the masters I've studied. I also gain strength from reading their biographies and learning how they struggled. They were always striving and never settled for good enough.

One important concept I learned from Glenn Vilppu is that a painting must entertain the eye. One of the ways is by controlling and directing the movement of the eye throughout the canvas. During

***Capriccio*. 54" × 48". Brushstrokes: 269. Year: 2006**

one of our trips to the art museums in Europe, Glenn taught us how the masters used nested curves to direct the viewer's eye movement across the canvas. Once you understand the concept, you'll easily recognize its application throughout art history. It certainly was a common practice in the work of the Italian Mannerists. Intrigued by this concept, I began playing with the curves. After a few dozen experimental drawings in my sketchbook, I came up with the idea for my *Capriccio* painting in 2006.

The inspiration for the color scheme of this painting came during a trip with Glenn and our art study group to the Anders Zorn art museum and his art studio in Mora, Sweden, a four-hour train ride north of Stockholm. Zorn used lots of browns and earth tones, with greens and often a small splash of red. During the same European trip, we also visited the art museum in Copenhagen. While looking at a small Edgar Degas painting with dancers on a stage, I saw a small splash of red in the lower left corner and another in the lower right corner. Glenn explained that your eye is naturally compelled to connect the two red areas, thus moving your view across the canvas. So I added this technique into the design. Then, further down on each side of the composition, I added an object at a forty-five-degree angle pointing outward. You'll sometimes see this in a Renaissance master's compositional design to open the image up. I also incorporated a couple of techniques used by Clyfford Still of the New York School, which I saw in his paintings in his museum in Denver. He'd often put an object next to the edge of the canvas or in the corner, creating visual tension, thus directing the eye to that part of the canvas.

For me, it was fun assembling and arranging these concepts into the design of my new painting. Interestingly, I know the artistic story of how these concepts evolved and then the technical story of how they were created. That's what I think of when I view *Capriccio*. It's somewhat surprising to me that it has become a favorite of many of my studio visitors, without them even knowing this background information.

Much like new artistic concepts I develop for each painting, I strive to do something that is technically different and challenging for each painting. I have experimented with and incorporated many exciting techniques and technologies, including many types of AI. As I've stated before, I will never copy a photograph, since that's not creative for me. Therefore, I always seek new ways to create something. The approach typically involves creating an artificial world inside the computer, using layers and layers of complex code.

On some mornings, before going into the studio, I used to stop at my favorite coffee shop, find a quiet area, and do some brainstorming or problem solving regarding a current painting project. At times like these, I would enter that distinctive flow state. The owner served coffee in a big round cup that looked more like a small cereal bowl. During one of these morning trips in 2013, I became fascinated by the swirling energy and motion of the milk in my cappuccino. I kept imagining what that energy might look like if captured in a large painting. After a few more coffee shop visits, I was energized and fascinated by what could become an exciting painting. I then had to figure out how to create it so the artistic and technical concepts were closely and sequentially coupled.

Now that I had the inspiration for my *Cappuccino* painting, I then had to solve the problem of how to create that swirling motion in the computer, capture that energy, and then convert that into brushstrokes. Filled with apprehension, I decided I needed to create a dynamic, swirling fluids simulator—an interesting subset of chaotic systems—and then mathematically capture that swirling motion.

When I was running the dynamic simulation, the fluids would hit the walls of the container and each other, resulting in swirling energy and motion. Inside the computer, this mathematical simulation created a visually dynamic and magical world. Excited, I spent weeks fine-tuning the simulator and adjusting all the parameters, creating hundreds of swirling fluid simulations. Finally, I found my keeper, which became the basis for an impressively large painting. But there was still much to do to create the eventual brushwork.

Biological systems are also a rich source of inspiration and offer examples for these simulated worlds. Think of the fascinating visual behavior patterns of schools of fish and flocks of birds. What about the collective, coordinating power of colonies of ants? Using colonies of simulated ants to create something new has become a favorite project of mine. We know real ants scurry around collecting food, building tunnels, caring for the young, and taking the

A close friend admiring some brushwork

garbage out. In a computer simulation and with a simple set of behavior rules, they have the power to interact with each other and their environment, known as stigmergy. As they wander around, I think of them laying down pebbles and building something. Then I collect and convert all those pebbles into brushstrokes, with the potential of creating exciting visual content for a painting. With each hit of the Run button, I get a new design. And, to my delight, they most often produce unanticipated and exciting results. As an example, the design of *Early Light*, seen near the end of this book (page 260), was laid out by my colonies of ants.

Every painting has its own story and unique evolution. I could use the same techniques repeatedly, but where's the fun in that? What's the point? Challenging myself and trying to push the limits for each new painting is what excites me. It allows me to venture into that wonderful, creative state of flow. Most important, it forever makes my journey so rich and rewarding.

I'm always evolving and following my passion to fuse art and science. The reason I choose to work on a painting instead of skiing

Cappuccino. 64″ × 86″. Brushstrokes: 2,956. Year: 2013

***Tadpoles.* 48" × 78". Brushstrokes: 996. Year: 2005**

or fly-fishing is the journey has become my passion, my *ikigai*, my reason for being. That's true self-fulfillment, and it's why I have evolved so far along my journey.

I'm reminded of my progress when I look at all the paintings I've created with Dulcinea that now hang on my gallery walls. While I don't do it often, I can sit back and appreciate how the process and the paintings have evolved over the years. I have rich memories of each one. They all have a unique story and serve as markers, benchmarks that show the gradual growth that has occurred along my journey. True to form, the next painting would be the most ambitious one I had ever attempted.

Solutions Only a Fusioneer Can Envision

After experiencing the tragic loss of someone close to me, I wanted to create a painting in her memory and to express my love. That was the inspiration for what would become *Meditation upon Death*.

But what's the painting's concept? What does it look like? I had no idea. We both grew up Catholic, so when you die, you either go "up there" or "down below." Instead of adopting a religious theme, I wondered if there was a spiritual concept I could capture.

A professional writer friend suggested, as a starting point, that I could think of the painting as if it were a story or a play in three acts. Okay, so perhaps act 1 would be the tragic moment of death, with acts 2 and 3 to follow. But then what would they be?

Out of the blue, a longtime friend and former nun turned schoolteacher invited me to a four-day workshop on Native American prayer, hosted in her home in Denver. A shaman would be leading the workshop and teaching us the practices of her own tribe. It wasn't anything I had any knowledge of or had expressed any interest in before, but I decided to go. That was a fortuitous decision. There were seven of us in the class. After each mini lecture, we were given a new prayer assignment and would individually venture into her backyard. We'd later meet up again in her living room to share our experiences. By the fourth day, I was sitting in the backyard, giving thanks to and talking to trees and bushes—a far cry from the physics I learned at Berkeley.

Everyone in the group had the opportunity to meet one-on-one with the shaman. During my time with her, I explained my tragic loss and the painting I was trying to develop. She became quite emotionally disturbed and then explained how when someone dies, their spirit goes through realms of the afterlife. Through prayer, the people in the tribe help the spirit move along. I thought her explanation had such a beautiful, upward-moving, visual quality to it. I knew in that moment what she'd described would be my inspiration for act 2, the journey of the spirit through realms of the afterlife.

I started working on acts 1 and 2, hoping the concept for act 3 would eventually reveal itself. For act 1, I struggled to capture the tragic moment of death, without it looking like a cliché. I filled numerous sketchbooks trying to capture that moment. I wanted this painting to take the viewer's breath away. I wanted the viewer to experience a special moment of quiet and introspection. Capturing tragedy in the moment of death was critical to the overall design.

Act 2 needed visual movement upward, representing the spirit wandering through the realms of the afterlife. This motion needed a meditative, graceful quality to it. How do you capture the essence of that? The nested curves. I filled additional sketchbooks, all with different emotional and visual effects. For instance, if the curves were too rounded, they would not convey the solemn, reserved nature of the journey. If they were too flat, the viewer would fly right up the curves through the realms of the painting too quickly. David Leffel taught that you want to control the rate at which the eye moves through a painting, so since this was a painting about meditation and death, that was a careful consideration.

After completing pages of notes and hundreds of sketches, I had a concise conceptual design in my head. I then started the coding process to create this three-act play of images on the computer. This would encompass layers and layers of code and many technical approaches. Months turned into years of work, but I still didn't have a final act 3. How did this spirit's journey through the realms end?

I spent months coding the robot to paint plumes of incense for act 3, only to abandon the effort after it wasn't fulfilling what I needed visually, so I continued developing acts 1 and 2. The concept for act 3 came to me near the end of the process, long after I had abandoned the incense idea. I wanted an unsettling ending. I liked the simplicity and quiet beauty of the three small, delicate curves that softly and quietly floated off into space in the upper-left corner of the painting.

The painting was sequentially developed in manageable sections. The coding and painting of act 1 went through many iterations. Dulcinea would paint only act 1 on a test canvas before the design, color, and brushwork would go through several more iterations. Sometimes it was a painstaking process. Was I capturing that tragic moment? Was the color working? What about improving

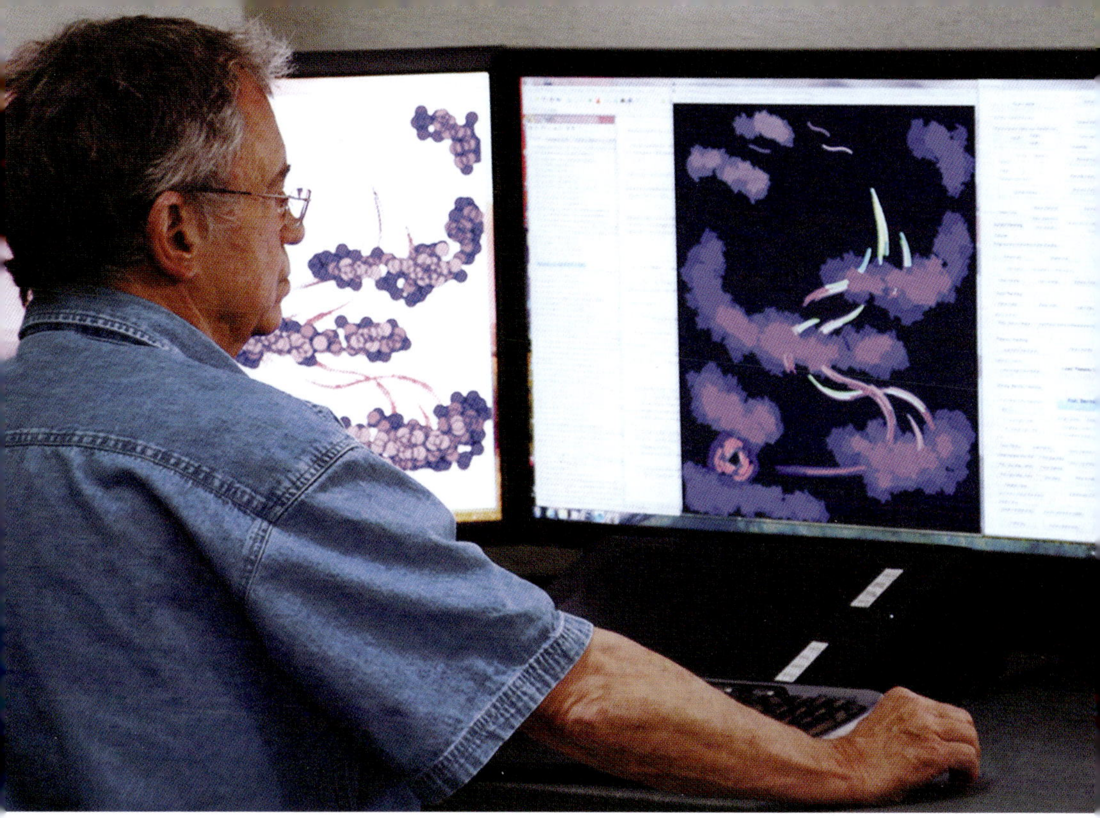

Paul in flow—a favorite place for him

the design? The brushwork? The thickness of the paint? The pressure of the brush on the canvas? Was the brushstroke capturing the artistic gesture I wanted? The list of questions went on and on.

Capturing the layering of clouds, representing the passages through realms, presented a unique set of problems. How do you apply light-colored paint on a dark background yet have it look soft, without any hard edges? How do you create that ethereal, cloud-like quality with a robot on a dark background? I used up rolls of canvas evolving this part of the painting.

The curves presented a different set of challenges. Along with the clouds, they were an essential element to the painting. For the painting to be successful, the spirit needed to appear to pass quietly and gracefully through the layers of clouds while moving through the realms of the afterlife. Capturing that movement relied upon your eye following nested curves, a technique I learned from Glenn Vilppu and successfully used in the *Capriccio* painting.

Swirling Timbers of Chaos. 66" × 60". Brushstrokes: 24,875. Year: 2010

When making a curving brushstroke, rather than using a typical flat artist's brush, it's better to use a round brush and continuously roll it throughout the stroke, taking fresh paint off the side of the brush as you go. I had Dulcinea emulate this brushstroke maneuver, and while it worked well, after a five- or six-inch stroke, it lacked sufficient paint, and the brushstroke became sketchy. I successfully used this technique with the round brush in the *Cappuccino* painting and a painting called *Swirling Timbers of Chaos*, and it worked well because the strokes weren't generally longer than six inches. However, I needed longer strokes to capture that graceful essence of the spirit's movement through the realms.

I had modeled Dulcinea's wrist after the human hand. I built her wrist so it would have a similar three-dimensional range of motion. An artist, using their wrist and elbow, can typically roll a brush with 180 degrees of rotation. Anything more than that isn't possible for an artist—or for Dulcinea, at least not at this time.

The solution I devised is an excellent example of how fusioneers have an advantage when it comes to solving certain problems. It's a result of having multiple skill sets and knowledge of multiple domains. What if I could continuously take paint off all sides of a round brush, facilitating a naturally longer curving brushstroke before running out of paint? What if I could continuously roll the brush 360 degrees, rather than just 180 degrees?

Since I built the wrist, I knew the motor used for rolling the brush could keep turning a full 360 degrees of rotation. Since I had configured the robot's operating system, I could make that adjustment accordingly. I wrote the code that ran the robot, so I could make that upgrade. I also wrote the code for the brushstrokes in the curves of the painting, so I could make those changes too. All of these points of view successfully came together very quickly.

It was a fusioneer's solution. Would an artist consider rolling the brush 360 degrees an option? Would the robotic wrist designer consider it if trying to emulate the human wrist? Would the robot's configured operating system include this? Without this modification, the robot's coding and the painting's brushstroke specifications couldn't use these changes. Behold the creative power of a fusioneer. When seeing these new elegant brushstrokes form the graceful curves in the painting, I instantly knew they expressed the essence I was seeking, the heart and soul of the painting.

Capturing the vision I had for *Meditation upon Death* presented another challenge that required me to evolve. Dulcinea's maximum working envelope on a canvas was a 54-by-48-inch area. For larger paintings, I typically slid the canvas left and then right to paint each half sequentially. Sometimes I divided a painting into quadrants, by sliding it up and down. *Meditation upon Death* was taller than anything I'd previously attempted, and it wouldn't fit vertically.

After some thought, I evolved to a tapestry design that allowed me to roll up the canvas at the top or bottom. At the top of Dulcinea's steel structure, I added a roller system and mounted it on its own horizontal rail system that could slide the rolled canvas left or right. With the roller system for extra-tall canvases and the rail system for wide canvases, I could easily manage large paintings.

Eager to try it out, I created a large fluids painting, using a technique similar to the *Cappuccino* painting, but much wider. Since it was a horizontal image, that presented an additional challenge. I couldn't put rollers on the top and side of the structure at the same time, so I decided to rotate the painting ninety degrees and paint it sideways. I only needed to change one line of code—swap *X* for *Y*—and it worked out perfectly.

Because of the size of the canvas, I had to work on the painting in three vertical sections. I would paint the left and then the right of this first third. Acrylic paint may dry quickly, but the brushstrokes had to harden before I could roll up the canvas or it would flatten the paint's texture. That's why I waited three days before painting the left and right halves of the middle section and then three

A close-up of the spirit passing through realms of the afterlife

more days before painting the final third. In my excitement to view it in its entirety, since I had only seen the painting one-third at a time, I forgot to have Dulcinea sign it. Despite its unusual origin story, that framed painting remains a favorite of many visitors to the studio. It just happens to be six feet tall and twelve feet wide.

With the initial use of the new roller system complete, I now had the experience and preparation I needed to complete *Meditation upon Death*. Because the curves of act 2 were so crucial, I wanted to paint them together without moving the canvas. So I modified my roller sequencing scheme and painted the large middle section of the painting that encompassed all of act 2's curves first. I then sequentially painted the four quadrants, minus the previously painted middle portion of each. As with all my large paintings, because of the way the brushstrokes are interlaced and overlap between sections, you never see any anomalies in the brushwork.

Meditation upon Death. 78″ × 68″. Brushstrokes: 5,796. Year: 2018

They blend together perfectly, but developing that algorithm did require some intense head scratching.

Meditation upon Death took me the better part of five years to complete. What kept me going was the opportunity to honor someone I had lost. Because of that, persistence came naturally. I loved what I was doing, so that created an inherent desire to strive and keep evolving until I fulfilled my vision for the painting. I have a shower stall filled with rolled canvases that remind me of the many stages of experimentation, critique, revision, and developmental iteration that went into the painting's creation.

That's inherently part of evolving. This painting represents the epitome of fusioneering. The solutions and innovations created during its Evolve phase extend beyond a single domain. These were solutions only a fusioneer with knowledge in the domains of art, science, programming, and robotics would be able to think of. If you can reach that level and use fusioneering and your knowledge of multiple domains to transcend what is currently possible, you can be a pioneer who creates something truly unique.

The dome of the Santa Maria del Fiore cathedral in Florence

CHAPTER 13

A Fusioneer Dreams

History is filled with examples of people doing the impossible. My favorite story is about Filippo Brunelleschi, who built the dome atop the Santa Maria del Fiore cathedral in Florence, Italy.

Construction began on the cathedral in 1296. The nearby towns of Pisa and Siena had recently built cathedrals, and the elites of Florence felt they needed an architectural masterpiece to match the grandeur of their city. And what better place to build the cathedral than in the heart of the city, where so much was happening intellectually and artistically?

The architect and sculptor Arnolfo di Cambio designed the structure and was hired to oversee the construction. He passed away ten years later, and the project stalled until the famed painter and architect Giotto took over in 1334. He passed away three years later, and then work was halted in 1348 due to the Black Death, leading to further delays. In 1367, an artistic committee decided upon a new design. It featured a dome 276 feet high and wider than the Pantheon in Rome at 143.5 feet. Cambio's original design also had a dome, but this one was much more ambitious. It would be the world's largest dome. The only thing that wasn't yet clear was how to build it.

Due to the octagonal shape and the enormous height and width of the dome, no one knew how to support the thousands of pounds of material during its construction. They didn't even know how to get the materials hundreds of feet into the air so the dome could be assembled. Despite what seemed impossible, the committee took a leap of faith and decided to move forward with the construction, even though it was unclear if what they imagined was architecturally possible. They were so driven to push beyond what the Romans had created and show what Florence as a society was capable of that they hoped future generations would discover a solution for how to build it.

After various delays, the construction of the massive cathedral neared completion in 1418, yet there was still no conceivable way to build its dome. So the city did what they often did when faced with near-impossible tasks; they turned to the people for help by hosting a competition. Anyone who could design a feasible solution was promised a significant cash prize two or three times more than the average artisan made in a year.

Filippo Brunelleschi was a goldsmith and a clockmaker by trade who designed one of the first alarm clocks. He was also a great thinker, artist, and fusioneer. He could have been a doctor, lawyer, or teacher, but he had an artist's sensibility and innate curiosity that led to him working with his hands. Brunelleschi had fared well in competitions before. In a 1401 competition, at age twenty-four, he designed a set of bronze doors for the Baptistery of San Giovanni, only to lose out to his rival, Lorenzo Ghiberti. Afterward, he left Florence and traveled to Rome, where he stayed for thirteen years, during which he spent time with Donatello and studied the ancient ruins.

Upon returning to Florence, Brunelleschi was one of twelve people who built models for the dome competition. He was already familiar with the project; his father had been on the 1367 committee that voted to take this leap of faith in the first place. There is a legend that when Brunelleschi made his presentation, he said they should give the commission to anyone who could balance an egg on its end. Nobody in the room could do it. Brunelleschi proceeded to crack the bottom of the egg to balance it upright. Someone said, "We could've done that if we'd thought of it." He responded, "And you could build a dome if you think like I do." It's just a legend and most likely didn't happen that way, but true or not, it encapsulates first-principles thinking and the ingenuity required to solve problems and break new ground.

Brunelleschi's model was radical and didn't use any centering or scaffolding at all. Some people thought he was crazy, but being well versed in multiple domains, his work was both innovative and impressive enough to win over the decision makers. A man with no architectural training, and with no precedent for his proposed construction, Brunelleschi was still declared the competition's winner, thus beginning his fusioneering journey.

It would be another year before construction started, in 1420. Brunelleschi is believed to have experimented extensively and perfected his design using large models. That was followed by a series of proposals and negotiations, which forced him to proceed cautiously. The first fifth of the dome needed to be built before he was allowed to continue. Those in charge wanted assurance that building a dome this size without any centering support was even possible, so his vision was questioned every step of the way.

It all began with the design. Given the massive width of the base, the dome couldn't be supported with a wooden framework or scaffolding because that required far too much wood and would have been extremely expensive. He wouldn't use any framework. Instead, he would create an inner and outer shell to the dome, one nested within the other. The inner shell was a series of self-supporting horizontal rings. The two shells were bound together with iron bars that functioned like the rings around a barrel.

This potentially solved one problem, but how do you build a dome and keep it stable as the inward slope and the downward pressure increase, the higher you get? Brunelleschi decided to use bricks instead of stone because they would be much lighter, but the masonry still needed to support itself. His solution was to place the bricks in a spiral, herringbone pattern, a design element he learned from Roman architecture. Each brick that was added locked the structure into place, preventing the dome from collapsing inward. This kept it stable during construction without the use of a wooden armature. Precise measurements and calculations were required to ensure that all eight sides of the dome's structure would successfully meet at the top. Eight teams of eleven builders were hired, one for each side of the octagon. They went to work six and sometimes seven days a week, weather permitting. It is believed that more than three hundred men worked on the construction of the dome.

Since there was no precedent for what Brunelleschi was trying to accomplish, obstacles constantly presented themselves, and he was continually forced to find solutions. The journey for Brunelleschi was one of continuous evolution and growth. Every new phase of the construction required a new invention. That forced him to call upon his knowledge of multiple domains to create fused solutions that pushed the limits of what was possible. When faced with the challenge of getting materials, and hundreds of 1,700-pound sandstone beams, to the construction site, and then onto the top of the cathedral, Brunelleschi created several cranes, pulley systems, and hoists, some as tall as sixty-five feet.

The most innovative and well-known creation was the ox hoist, which Brunelleschi invented and built in 1421. It was a hoist powered by oxen walking in a circle to turn the crank. When he realized that oxen didn't like to back up, preventing the hoist from moving in reverse, he created the world's first clutch mechanism. This way, the ox could walk in the same direction while the hoist changed direction. The hoist raised an average of fifty loads a day, one every ten minutes. This impressive feat of fusioneering and creativity required knowledge in the domains of math, engineering, carpentry, materials, husbandry, and design. The result was a hoist system that was stronger and more powerful than any that had come before.

For the hoist to work as intended, the rope needed to be especially strong. It was ordered from the shipbuilding town of Pisa, where they had perfected advanced rope-making techniques. However, the hoist created so much friction that it became a fire hazard, so the rope was doused with water to prevent it from catching fire as it passed through the pulley wheels. The machine and clutch were centuries ahead of their time, and the ox hoist remains one of the most celebrated inventions of the Renaissance.

It's understood that, during the Evolve phase, issues and problems will arise. Sometimes ideas won't work out. Brunelleschi's journey was no exception. To speed up the delivery of marble (which was needed for the ribs of the dome) from the northern city of Carrara, he created a boat called *Il Badalone*, so the material could be transported down the Arno River instead of by donkey. The design was patented in 1421, but the ship sank, so the remaining marble ended up being transported on land via donkey.

Despite his periodic failures, what emerged from this period were several innovative, never-before-seen solutions to complex problems, large and small. For example, the builders were working up in the cramped quarters of the dome from dawn until dusk almost every day. To save the workers from continuously making the long trek up and down the stairs to eat, Brunelleschi installed a small kitchen up in the working area of the dome in 1426 so they could cook their noon meals.

Throughout the construction process, Brunelleschi maintained control over every phase and didn't divulge his methods out of fear of being replaced. It's believed that the ox hoist was built by different groups of workmen who were kept in the dark about what the other groups were doing. This secrecy ensured that he would remain essential to the process and that his name would be forever attached to the dome. That also meant he needed to work quickly if he wanted to see his work completed in his lifetime. However, there were a series of complications that caused further setbacks and threatened the dome's completion.

As I mentioned earlier, Brunelleschi's design was questioned every step of the way because it remained uncertain whether what he was attempting was even possible. In 1429, those doubters seemed temporarily vindicated when cracks began to appear in the dome. Faced with yet another problem, Brunelleschi's solution was to build a ring of individual chapels around the outside base of the cathedral to provide additional support for the cathedral's walls.

The following year, Florence went to war with the nearby city of Lucca, and Brunelleschi was recruited for military architecture commissions. This pulled him away from his work on the dome. As part of the war effort, he designed and built a dam to deflect the Arno River, but it proved to be a disaster, and he took the blame for the army's defeat. Meanwhile, workers on the dome saw their wages cut during the war effort. Right when it looked like Brunelleschi had removed all the impediments standing between him and completion of the dome, he was arrested in 1434 for failing to pay dues to the mason guild in what was believed to be a political prosecution. When he was released, he resumed work.

After constant evolution, growth, and development, the project was finally completed in 1436, sixteen years after Brunelleschi began construction. The dome contains more than four million bricks that weigh more than 40,000 tons. It stands 276 feet high, the same height as the Statue of Liberty. It became the new hub of the city, ripe with new possibilities. When Brunelleschi died in 1446, ten years later, he left behind no sketches or writings about his methods. We have no way of knowing exactly what he did or how he knew what he knew. Many experts have speculated and since figured out some techniques, but much of how it was done remains a mystery. Driven by his self-belief and a daring ability to break new ground, he set a new standard within the domains of art, architecture, and engineering. Instead of continuing to be associated with manual laborers, the role of the architect was elevated in social and intellectual circles. Arguably, more important than anything else, he helped to broaden people's thinking and redefine what was possible.

Brunelleschi inspired generations of Renaissance artists and thinkers that followed. One in particular was Leonardo da Vinci. As we noted earlier, while serving as an apprentice under Verrocchio, da Vinci was part of the group of artists who designed, built, and installed the copper ball on top of Brunelleschi's dome in 1471. They even used Brunelleschi's ox hoist to do so, and Leonardo's drawings of the machinery have become famous.

The iconic dome atop Florence's Santa Maria del Fiore cathedral has survived earthquakes, lightning, and war. It's still standing today, and you can still climb the 463 steps that Brunelleschi and his workers climbed every day to work. It remains the largest masonry dome in the world and one of the greatest engineering feats of all time. And it was created during a period when it should have been impossible, given the technology available at the time.

Growth during the Evolve phase can come in many forms, but when in pursuit of your passion and doing what you love, you will thrive on creating innovative solutions that have the potential to transform your work. You may even accomplish things you never thought possible when you first set out on your journey.

The Journey Is Ongoing

Upon completing one painting, I'm eager to start the next one. The process is ongoing for me. That is the nature of the journey and what I find so thrilling.

After completing *Meditation upon Death,* I carefully went through several conceptual genres before selecting the idea for my next painting. Fascinated by the Hubble and James Webb telescopes, I thought about looking into deep space and capturing thousands of points of light, such as within a swirling plasma field. I spent months pursuing and coding ideas and discovered that it was doable. I could see it on the screen, but while it was intellectually intriguing, something was missing.

I knew for this next concept that I wanted to create something peaceful and quiet, given all the tension in our civil discourse at the time. I studied the ink and brush paintings of eighteenth-century Japanese Buddhist monks. In addition to the overall look and feel, I liked the gestural quality of the black-ink brushwork. Could I get Dulcinea to do something like that? I spent months exploring, sketching, and coding those possibilities.

Early Light. 23" × 88". Brushstrokes: 744. Year: 2023

Then I spent time exploring other ideas but still found I was not ready to commit to any of them yet. Meanwhile, as I indulged my habit of working out ideas in the early predawn with a cup of coffee, the view to the east out my sliding door that overlooked the lake kept capturing my attention. After repeatedly taking in this luminous view of sky and open space, as far as I could see, I began to deeply appreciate its sublime beauty, especially in the predawn light. That got me wondering: *Could I capture this awe-inspiring, soft, luminous light in a painting?* It would certainly be unlike anything I'd attempted before. My intention was not to create a sunrise landscape but an abstract painting that captured that early, predawn moment of quiet, sublime beauty.

With this inspiration for a new painting concept, I used my iPad Pro to gather a large collection of pictures, both before and after dawn, over several months. There was such a rich variety of images, colors, and textures. Some had deep, dramatic color with layers of dark clouds. Others were rather quiet and captured the calm, predawn stillness.

I studied the works of the English painter J. M. W. Turner and attempted to understand how he captured that luminous glow. I studied other artists as well but was never satisfied with what I saw. Turning back to Turner, who is arguably considered the greatest British painter, I was struck by his heavy reliance on layers and layers of thin glazes and paint applied on top of each other. This is how he achieved the soft, luminous effects he wanted. Having studied Turner's techniques and solidified my overall concept, I started experimenting with colors, their chroma and values, and brushwork, along with the overall design of the painting. Having my distilled, concise concept at hand, the stack of experimental test canvases continued to grow as the painting and my skill evolved.

No matter what your vision may be, evolving is essential to your journey. By its very nature, it's an ongoing process of expanding, exploring, trying, failing, and creating. Fusioneering is about this process, not the finished product. The goal is to pursue your vision while continually evolving and growing along your journey and not just get to the finish line. Sarah, Noah, and Tom are wonderful examples of this process.

The journey can be a struggle at times, but there is nothing else like it. It all goes back to your Seven Stories, innate intelligences, self-fulfilling dharma, true calling, and *ikigai*. When you can tap into what lights you up inside, it will provide you with energy as you work your way through the FUSE framework. When that occurs, and your vision is directly connected to your reason for being, you will feel true joy and fulfillment. You're living the dream!

Acknowledgments

Every fusioneer will need teachers or mentors along the way, especially in their Upgrade stage.

While attending art classes and workshops at the art school across the parking lot from my art studio, I was able to study with several art teachers. However, none were as valuable and generous with their knowledge as David Leffel and Glenn Vilppu, to whom I will be forever grateful.

Although I've evolved to a point well down my fusioneering path now, starting out can be very intimidating. Two robotics friends who were invaluable in the early days were Brain Carlisle, CEO at Adept Technology at the time, and Glenn Helmes, my *Have Gun Will Travel* traveling robotics consultant and hero who led me out of some difficult conundrums.

I'd also like to acknowledge my sister, for always being there for me, and my parents, for their love, warmth, and nurturing support, throughout my life, until their passing.

Index

D

E

F

G

H

I

J

K

L

M

N

O

P

R

S

T

U

V

About the Author

Although he was not aware of it, Paul has been living the FUSE model since 1977. While earning an electrical engineering degree at UC Berkeley, he applied for and was accepted into their ROTC program. Upon graduating in 1972, he was commissioned an officer in the US Air Force and served four years during the later part of the Vietnam War. While working in an Air Force research lab he was awarded two commendation medals.

After taking a self-assessment test in his second year of the MBA program at the Harvard Business School, he scored high in theoretical, which was not a surprise, but he also scored high in esthetic, which *was* a surprise. The other attributes were clustered much lower. Puzzling with what to do with this assessment and a future career path, and while walking on a footbridge across the Charles River on the evening of October 23, 1977, he was struck with the idea to combine technology and art and build a robot that paints. That was the first of three profound moments for him.

During the weekends of 1980–1981, Paul built his first painting robot while working in product marketing at a division of Hewlett-Packard. He later went on to have a successful career in venture capital. After retiring, and wondering what to do, he experienced his second profound moment in 1994. While on a skiing trip in Europe, he visited a Leonardo da Vinci museum exhibit. Walking out, and overwhelmed with what he had seen, he knew at that moment it was time to pursue his original dream—the fusion of art and science.

Paul then spent the next twenty-five years on his fusioneering journey, happily building his robot, Dulcinea, and together creating many paintings. Unknowingly, the third profound "moment" was about to occur. He was overwhelmed with the intensity and excitement exhibited by gifted fourth and fifth graders and at-risk high school kids visiting his studio.

He realized he had been given many gifts and that he had a deep responsibility to give back, to share what he'd done, and to excite and inspire others to pursue their own dreams. An outgrowth of that was the formulation of this FUSE framework—one he had lived—and this book. He hopes you too are inspired to find your pathway and lead a rich and fulfilling life as you were meant to.